KEY PERSON OF INFLUENCE

KEY PERSON OF INFLUENCE

The Five-Step Method to become one of the most
highly valued and highly paid people in your industry

DANIEL PRIESTLEY AND **MIKE REID**

RETHINK PRESS

First published in Great Britain 2014
by Rethink Press (www.rethinkpress.com)
This edition published in Canada in 2019

Cover image © Dent Global Limited

Illustrations: Andrew Priestley

PRAISE

"This book distills the principles for becoming a visible leader in your industry into five steps almost any entrepreneur can follow. It's simple, powerful and has worked extremely well for me."

Nicole Verkindt
Dragon on CBC's Next Gen Den, Next Gen Member of the Canadian Business Council and Founder of OMX

"KPI is to personal branding what Jim Collins' 'flywheel principle' was to making businesses great."

Jayson Gaignard
Canadian Entrepreneur, Author, Super-connector, and Founder of Mastermind Talks

"Leveraging your personal brand is one of the most effective strategies any small business owner can use to outperform their competitors today. If you want to cut through the noise, the KPI Method gives you a roadmap."

Rachel David
YouTuber, Instagram Influencer, and Founder of Hashtag Communications

"The KPI Method outlines a core purpose every entrepreneur should have. If you want to have an impact in the world, you must share it with the world. This book shows you how to rise above the noise and do just that."

Phillip Haid
Founder and CEO, PUBLIC Inc.

"This book has very powerful ideas that will have you achieving much more in far less time. Hard work is not enough; if you want to make it big, you must strive to become a Key Person of Influence. This book shows you exactly how to do that faster."

Mike Harris
Creator of three multi-billion-pound businesses and Author of Find Your Lightbulb

CONTENTS

We dedicate this book to the people who use their power of influence to improve the world.

We hope that the ideas in this book assist you in creating a world that works for everyone.

ABOUT THE CANADIAN EDITION

In 2010, Daniel Priestley released the book *Become a Key Person of Influence*. Never did we think that in such a short space of time it would become such a popular book among so many people. Since releasing the first edition, more than 100,000 entrepreneurs around the world have taken up a copy.

The five-step KPI Method outlined in the book focuses on helping entrepreneurs improve their skills in five cornerstone business areas: Pitch, Publish, Product, Profile, and Partnerships.

I've seen the KPI Method applied in more than fifty industries in the UK, the USA, Singapore, Australia, and now Canada. This simple but effective method for helping entrepreneurs to stand out, scale up, and make a real impact in their industry has struck a chord with a lot of people. As a result of the book, entrepreneurs have been getting out and pitching for bigger deals—and winning them.

Remarkably, the book has inspired hundreds of people to write their own books as well. Our office shelves are full of books people have written and sent us as a result of reading this book. Shockingly, we're up to nearly 1000 and counting.

I love discovering new products that people have created as a result of this book. I've seen people innovating product offerings ranging from scones in England to power boats in Australia. I've seen people who were stuck trading time for money start to turn their valuable insights into hot products that can be delivered worldwide.

On a regular basis I discover that someone with a high profile has used the KPI Method, too. People with millions of views online or regular TV appearances, high-profile speakers, and entertainers have described how the KPI Method has helped them go to the next level.

It's exciting to see entrepreneurs collaborating by sharing and expanding their resources through partnerships. People are approaching partnerships with the right intent and achieving more in a few months than they had in previous years. Powerful products, promotions, and even new companies are being created thanks to the spirit of partnership.

By far the best part of this story is watching the Key Person of Influence community spring up around the globe. In the UK, Australia, the USA, Singapore, and other countries, there's a thriving community of entrepreneurs and leaders who are using the KPI Method to make the most of the times we are in. I believe that we're in exciting, transformational times and there's never been more opportunity for people to have a big impact with their business or their message.

This Canadian edition was released in 2019 and features updated content, case studies, and local examples. If you're reading this book for the first time, you've stepped into something that's producing real results for a lot of people. Enjoy the book, join in with others who are using the method and share your experience with the world.

As for me, I left Australia in 2018 to help launch the KPI Method in Canada. Over the last eight years I've been helping grow the Key Person of Influence community in Australia to over 1000 entrepreneurs who are winning awards, adding six- and seven-figure products to their businesses, appearing in international media and being invited to speak at conferences like TEDx. I couldn't be prouder of what this extraordinary community is achieving around the globe.

I hope this book inspires you to stand out, scale up, and make a Dent in the universe. There's never been a better time to accelerate your journey.

Cheers,

Mike Reid

A TECHNICAL NOTE

While the first edition of this book was written by Daniel Priestley, this Canadian edition has been updated and revised by both the authors.

When we refer to "we," "I" or "Daniel and/or Mike," both authors have contributed to the contents of this edition and therefore the book can be read from either author's "voice."

INTRODUCTION

At the centre of every industry you will find an inner circle of people who are the most well-known and highly valued people. They are the "Key People of Influence."

You probably already know of these people in your industry:

- Their names come up in conversation… for all the right reasons.
- They attract a lot of opportunities… that are perfect for them.
- They earn more money than most… and it isn't a struggle.
- They can make a project successful if they are involved… and people know it.

Key People of Influence enjoy a special status in their chosen field because they are well connected, well-known, well regarded, and highly valued. They get invited to be a part of the best teams and projects, and they can often write their own terms.

Key People of Influence also have more fun. They get invited on trips away. People buy them dinner and drinks and give them VIP treatment. They are treated with respect, and others listen when they speak.

These people are in demand; they don't chase opportunities, they curate them.

People think that it must take years or decades to become a Key Person of Influence (KPI). They think that KPIs need degrees or doctorates. They think KPIs must be gifted or from a wealthy family.

While time invested, qualifications, talents, and a wealthy family are helpful, they are not a reliable way to make yourself a Key Person of Influence.

There are plenty of people who have been in an industry for years who are *not* Key People of Influence. There are plenty of MBAs and PhDs who are not yet KPIs. There are people with talent and people born into privileged families who aren't KPIs either.

And then there are the unusual stories like Daniel's.

Daniel arrived in the UK with little more than a suitcase and a credit card in 2006. He knew no one, and he didn't have a big budget to start our business.

Within a year, people started calling him one of the most connected entrepreneurs in London. Along with his partners, he built a business turning over millions, and he could get on the phone to any of the other high-flyers and heavy-hitters in his industry within a few calls.

All this in London—a big city that is known for being difficult in terms of breaking into the established networks. He was told it would take years to be accepted into the right circles and he was unlikely to be given any special treatment. He was told that London is a difficult city in which to achieve success in a short space of time.

How wrong the critics were. London works like any other city in the world because it is full of people, and people everywhere respond to the ideas we talk about in this book.

People all over the world respond to the method we will discuss in the coming chapters. It's a method based on clearly communicating your value and packaging it in a way the market finds desirable. The principles in this book have been tested across more than fifty different industries, in over a dozen countries, by over 3000 entrepreneurs and leaders; they have proven to be universal.

It's not difficult to become a Key Person of Influence within your industry in the next twelve months if you take the steps set out in this book, in the order they are prescribed, and you implement them at a high standard.

If you do, you won't need to do more university training or spend decades developing more technical skills. You will become a Key Person of Influence in your field very quickly.

THE HIDDEN THEME

This book contains powerful ideas and the chapters are set out in a particular order for a reason. We're going to give you a five-step method that will fast-track you toward "KPI status." The theme is pretty obvious.

Behind the obvious theme of this book and the five-step KPI Method, though, there is a hidden theme. There is a story behind the story, you could say. It's more powerful than anything we say in this book overtly. It's not a secret, but it's still hidden from most people.

When it becomes obvious to you, you will recognize it with a gut reaction. This hidden theme will click a lot of ideas into place quickly, and it will trigger a rush of energy and insights. You might sit up through the night "working" and still not be tired.

If you spot this hidden theme, you will find it easy to earn more money and you will discover some very exciting trends that are already close to your heart. Your future will become crystal clear and you will know your next steps.

This theme is hidden from most people only because they are too close to it. It's worth taking the time to discover it, though. Maybe you will discover it the first time you read this book, maybe on the fifth time. Maybe it will hit you in the shower one morning and then you will re-read this book to confirm it.

Either way, don't give up on getting the real message; all the juice is in "the story behind the story." It's the chapters that you haven't examined that will point the way.

You might think that the chapters are out of order, or that there are too many or too few. You might think that we haven't told you about the chapters you haven't seen yet. None of this is the case.

All the chapters are there for you to explore, and when you can connect the dots you will step into the realm of the true KPI.

You will never fear not having money or influence again.

You will already have everything you will ever need.

1

THE WORLD HAS CHANGED AND SO MUST YOU

We are living in a very different world today than we were just a decade ago. We're at the beginning of a whole new era.

We are no longer in the Industrial Age; we are in a new economy that's digital, global, intangible, more meaningful, and very entrepreneurial. Everything has changed and so must you.

LOOKING GOOD, GOING NOWHERE

I know an accountant; he is a great accountant. However, he's not happy and I know why. When he was eighteen years old, fresh out of high school, his best thinking was to study for this job. He was good at math and economics and, for all the right reasons, it made sense at the time to study and get into the accountancy profession.

Today he's frustrated. He's brilliant at what he does, but he still has to compete on price. Like most of the people in his industry, he thinks that the key to making more money is doing more study on the technical aspects of his job. Unfortunately for him, everyone in his line of work is focused on getting more qualifications, and he finds himself constantly playing catch-up. Regardless of how much he earns, he still feels that he is only slightly ahead of the game.

Lately he's been questioning everything: he feels that his life today is based upon the best thinking of his eighteen-year-old self; he has lived out twenty years of a teenager's decision; now he's in his late-thirties his values have shifted and so has the world.

He now competes with software, with accountants in India and with his own mindset about how his industry "should be."

His story isn't unique; I hear it all the time. Many people are great at what they do, but aren't fulfilled. The feeling creeps in that life is passing by too quickly and the goals you once had haven't been realized. You might even start questioning whether you made the right career choices; you might get frustrated with your industry or with life. You might even begin to resent people who are doing better than you.

By the end of this book, you are going to see that you don't need to turn your life upside down. You don't need to do more study or gain more technical expertise in your field. You can forget the MBA, if you want. You can also forget the get-rich-quick schemes that take you off track.

If you follow what I am about to tell you in this book, you will become a Key Person of Influence in your industry within the next twelve months. You'll enjoy yourself more, you'll make more money and it won't take you more time. You will even feel more sure of yourself.

As a KPI you'll do less of the functional work that wears you out and you'll do more of the dynamic, creative, and strategic activity that energizes you.

You'll become known for something unique. As a result of having a reputation within your niche you'll be more in demand. You'll spend less time chasing and more time fielding inbound enquiries.

Rather than trading your own time for money, you'll make money from products and services that you choose to represent. You'll have more people supporting you and you'll have highly effective partnerships that help make your ideas a reality.

However, before I begin to share with you some of the actions that need to be taken, we must first face up to some facts. We are living in a different world. It's not the same as it used to be. There are some new concepts you need to embrace and some old ideas you need to let go of quickly.

If you are willing to do that, then let's begin the journey.

YOUR BEST THINKING FIVE YEARS AGO IS YOUR BAGGAGE TODAY

In the last decade we have seen the explosive growth of new technology like social media, smart phones, automation, e-commerce, speech recognition, and freely available information at your fingertips.

We also witnessed a global recession and a massive shift toward entrepreneurship over employment. Talented people have changed the ways they live and work. Thanks to these bright minds, the world of business is more competitive than ever.

In the last few years we have seen the economy change, the environment change, developing nations stride forward, and the collective mindset of the world radically shift. All in just a few short years.

It's safe to assume your best thinking from five years ago is your outdated baggage today.

Any decisions you made back then about your business or career, your location, the technology you use, the people you associate with, and the thought leaders you follow are all based upon a world that no longer exists.

Software I purchased five years ago for $10k+ has been superseded by free, cloud-based software, and what I dreamed of doing five years ago now costs only $100 a month!

Entrepreneurs I admired five years ago who didn't shift their business model have lost their fortunes. Many experts of five years ago are now scratching their heads. Great leaders from five years ago now have teams who aren't performing.

Customers expect to get for free the things they would have paid highly for five years ago. Products that used to be available only through retail are now freely available online.

The countries that offered the best opportunities for wealth creation five years ago are struggling with debt. The poor countries of the previous decade are the powerhouses of tomorrow's free markets.

Unless we can let go of everything we currently think and do, we will fail to see the opportunities of tomorrow. The temptation, however, is to throw everything away—the baby with the bathwater. At the core of who you are and what you do, though, is a raw essence that has always powered you. You need to strip back to that core and create new ways to express it.

When Steve Jobs took over Apple in 1997, one of his first decisions was to get rid of the Apple Museum that occupied the foyer where people walked through the front door. He said that he refused to be in a company that was living in its past. He believed at the core of Apple was vision, boldness, and innovation. He knew the essence of Apple was thinking differently and combining art with technology. If he couldn't strip away everything but that, the future was going to be dire.

It's time to draw a line in the sand, take some time out, and ask yourself what is at *your* core. Ask yourself this question:

> *"If I was starting completely fresh, in a world where anything is possible, what would I love to be doing?"*

I haven't asked you what you should be doing. I've asked you what you would love to be doing. If you are like most people, your passionate purpose is a lot closer than you think. There are parts of your business that you love, parts that drain your energy, and maybe even parts you hate. Maybe you have a passion you love but the business you hate keeps you from it; look for the clues that are hidden in that passion.

This book will reveal to you exactly how you can position yourself as a Key Person of Influence (KPI) in your field within the next twelve months. As a result you will attract opportunities, connections, ideas, and resources that mean you will be able to do what you love and get paid what you are worth.

In this new, exciting, changing world, you will discover that the people and teams who are doing what they love are the ones who are thriving. If it feels like hard work you will always get trumped by those who have passion.

Your passion and vitality are an asset in the world we are living in, so let's take a look at what lights you up.

EXERCISES

- What comes easy to you that is harder for others?
- If you got to do a month of fully paid "work experience" in any industry, job, business or hobby, what would you do?
- If you or your team had to apply your skills to something purely for the fun of it, what project would you like to work on?
- What did you discover about yourself when you answered these questions?

NOTES ...

VITALITY IS MORE VALUABLE THAN FUNCTIONALITY

Key People of Influence are vital people, not functional people.

You can't get the results you want without a vital person because they add something a functional person doesn't have.

Functional people might be great at what they do, they might talk the talk and walk the walk, but the harsh reality is they are performing a role that is replaceable. If someone can find a cheaper option they will take it, because a functional person is just one possible solution to a problem.

A company can downsize functional people. A client can replace a functional supplier. An investor can easily put their money into someone else. Functional does the job, but functional is still interchangeable.

People who are functional see themselves as competent when executing a set of processes. They try to get better at those processes and they make marginal improvements. Secretly, they like the status quo and resist change or disruptive thinking.

People who are performing a vital role see themselves as aligned to the result rather than the process. They ask questions about "why" things are done in a particular way and challenge the process in pursuit of something better. They're obsessed with delivering value and are willing to let go of old patterns of thinking to achieve it.

The word "vital" has two potent definitions. One definition means "irreplaceable" and the other means "life-force." Vital people see themselves as being the "irreplaceable life-force" of a project, a business, an industry or even a cause.

They feel as if they own a specific piece of turf and that no one could replace them; any new people who show up are potentially new partners, not competitors. They see themselves as redefining the game in some way. They have their own unique take on things that makes them almost impossible to overlook.

Functional people are scared to take a vacation. They worry about what will happen while they are gone. Will they have a business to come back to? Will their clients find someone else? Will they lose opportunities they really need? A vacation is a scary thing when you are performing a functional role.

Vital people love taking vacations. They know that's part of what makes them vital. They have a unique spark and fresh ideas that people want to tap into. For a vital person, a vacation is a time to get re-energized and to stimulate ideas. It's also a great reminder to everyone just how vital they are. A vital person knows that while they are gone, people are worried that they won't come back.

Functional people feel relieved to associate with people who reaffirm that life is tough. They like to be reassured that the economy is affecting others too and that times aren't what they used to be. A functional person loves the comfort of their friends who don't push them or inspire them to step up to a whole new level.

A vital person likes to be seen by their contemporaries. They welcome challenging debate and stimulating ideas. They happily engage in retraining themselves and evolving with changing trends.

They want people to push them, to bring out the best in them, and to stay true to the idea that there's always a new level to play at. A vital person will leave a group of people that slows them down for a group that stirs them up.

You can choose to become more of a functional person or a vital person. You can focus on being busy or on getting results. You can choose to take a stand for the way things are done or the way things could be done. You can be highly capable or highly irreplaceable.

A functional person wants to get more; a vital person wants to produce more.

A functional person wants to learn more; a vital person wants to share more.

A functional person wants to be shown a path; a vital person wants to create one.

A functional person is worn out by their functionality; a vital person is re-energized by their vitality.

The choice is yours from this moment forward; you can choose how you want to show up.

EXERCISES

- Who do you know who shows up as a functional person?
- Who do you know who is currently a vital person?
- What are some of the differences you notice between them?

NOTES ...

YOUR CAREER IS OVER

A career is "old technology." It was a great way to structure work for many years. It was an efficient way to get a return on the investment of training and developing staff.

That world is over. Today the world expects you to be trained, to educate yourself constantly, and to bring something new to the table. For that reason, talented people move around and "career workers" become highly vulnerable.

If you are in business, don't think that you are safe. With the speed at which things are moving today, your business is going to have to reinvent itself constantly. As an entrepreneur, almost every two years you'll need to sit down and dream up a whole new plan for what you do and how you do it. If you don't, you'll be overtaken by those who do.

So if there's no security in jobs any more, and if small businesses are constantly changing, how do you secure your income and your business?

Through your personal brand.

Today, your most valuable asset is the number of people who know you, like you and trust you. You are already being defined by your unique take on things, your story, and your ability to innovate. This is happening whether you choose to actively participate or not.

Every opportunity will involve a Google search of your personal brand. Every team you lead will be based on your story, not your CV. Every deal that makes you richer will be because of who you are, not what it says on your business card.

In the future you will discover that what you do might change, but your core passion only becomes stronger because everything you do reinforces a central theme.

From now on you must see yourself as being in an enterprise that others need to know about.

Your business needs to become known for something unique. It's not enough just to offer a service at a fair price. You need to build a brand, develop your own intellectual property, accumulate stories, and claim a leadership role within your niche.

You won't be known for just your company's name; you will be known for the people you're connected to, the ideas you are immersed in, and what you care deeply about. Once these things are more widely known, you will have a constant stream of opportunities coming your way from places you've never been.

Your career as you know it may be dead, but if you position yourself as a Key Person of Influence your adventure is just beginning.

THE HARDER YOU WORK, THE LESS YOU EARN

In the modern economy, hard work is not a competitive advantage anymore; everyone works hard.

If you were to gather up all the hardest-working people in the world, you would not find the top CEOs and the entrepreneurs; you would find the people who are struggling to make it up the ladder or struggling to survive at all.

The competitive advantage is in thinking expansively, connecting with the right people, and spotting fresh opportunities.

Your best ideas will come out to play... not to work.

With that in mind, a week of skiing with friends in Alberta could yield you more ideas, connections, and perspective than a week of answering emails, catching up on paperwork, and attending meetings.

As we discussed, the difference between the successful and unsuccessful people on the planet is not functionality, it's vitality. Functionality is about performing a task well, whereas vitality requires you to be energized and joyful.

In the last ten years we have seen machines and systems replace a whole lot of functionality in the workplace; however, we are a long, long way from seeing the first machine that can compete with raw human vitality.

Vitality yields creativity and innovation. It yields leadership. It yields boldness and robustness under pressure. It yields insights and breakthroughs. Software and machinery can't do that; software and machinery can only do the stuff that we call work.

If you look at the top earners, they don't consider what they do to be work. They are playing a game that they love, and they make sure that it stays fun. They exude a level of vitality for what they do and because they love it, they get good at it too.

The minute you begin to feel yourself "working hard" as opposed to "playing a challenging game" it's time to take a break or get around some new people. Disappear for a week, get some sun, read up on your favourite role models, explore fresh ideas, and spend time with people who are "in their zone." Attend a new event, read a new book, and have a few new conversations.

More than anything, reconnect with your humanity. Beneath your desire to have a great home, a snappy wardrobe, and some money in the bank is a part of you that longs to make a difference as well. Getting in touch with this part of you will give you a broadband connection to your vitality.

From a place of vitality all the work comes easily, the ideas flow freely and the money comes in more effortlessly. An hour of inspiration is worth more than a week of drudging on. A day of creativity will do more for your career or business than a month of hard work.

Success isn't about engaging in a struggle; it is about getting into your flow.

You can't expect things to change if you're not willing to get out of your comfort zone. You need to surround yourself with fresh ideas, insightful people, and inspiring places. You need to be part of a peer group that holds you to a higher standard.

One of the clients we worked with redesigned his business so he could live anywhere in the world and work four days per week. He thought that he would earn less than before, but in reality he's become more highly valued and highly paid. He lives in a large homestead an hour out of the city, and a top-performing team come to him (and love it).

You owe it to yourself to stop working so hard and to start living your life in a way that lights up yourself and others.

EXERCISES

Here are a couple of great questions you might want to explore:

- What would you love to do this week if you couldn't work?
- Who would you love to spend more time with who you don't normally see?
- Where would you love to spend time this week if you wanted to be more creative and adventurous?
- How would you deliver more value to others if you didn't need to worry about your schedule or commitments?
- What difference would you love to make on the planet if you could just give your time and talent more freely?

NOTES ...

DIGITAL CHANGED EVERYTHING

The digital revolution has changed everything. New opportunities and challenges are emerging every day.

People have integrated technology into the fabric of their lives. It's hard to imagine a week without your smart phone, wi-fi or social networks. People are rapidly connecting the dots with all this technology and finding new and transformational ways to stitch it all together.

One thing we know for sure is whenever there are new and powerful ways to connect, they have a huge impact on business.

It's now possible for a seventeen-year old girl sitting in her bedroom to start a group on Facebook for free. She can have thousands of followers and fans worldwide for free. She can talk to them all on video for free. She can write to them all for free. She can get them all excited about her ideas... all without spending any of her money.

This teenager can create or source a product easily and cheaply. She can design a brand easily and cheaply. She can have an online-store easily and cheaply. She can take payment easily and cheaply.

She can send her products whizzing around the world easily and cheaply... All from her bedroom.

Most people think that these "whiz kids" are succeeding because they are good with technology, but this is not the whole story.

These teenagers aren't attached to the idea that a business has to be the way it used to be. They don't think a brand needs to cost a lot of money or that they need to live in a particular location in order to do business there. They don't think that their idea needs to please everyone or that they need to meet their clients face-to-face in order to deliver a powerful experience.

That's why they are succeeding: not because they are better at using the technology, but because they are better at letting go of the way things were done in the past and probably because they were never attached to these ideas in the first place.

REVOLUTIONARY STUFF

The game has fundamentally changed. The internet, social media, mobile, wearables, voice recognition, cheap processing power in everyone's pocket, the internet of things: it will change everything. Every industry, every job, every business, every life on the planet.

It's just like when the combustion engine came along and the game changed. The Industrial Revolution introduced new technology that changed everything for people in the agricultural age. The people who used machines made fortunes and the people who stuck to their old ways ended up on the factory floor.

New, global, small teams can also deliver high quality at a lower cost in many niches. Small teams can source products and ideas faster and more cheaply over the internet than big businesses can. Small enterprises can access big factories when they need to but don't have the overheads when they aren't using them. Small runs lean but powerful in this economy.

Small can look very big now.

Best of all, small cares about you, the individual.

If you are a vegetarian and you want to go to the gym, you can learn from the world's best vegetarian bodybuilder. He could give you recipes, workout routines, and products made just for vegetarian bodybuilders, and you could see every meal he eats on Instagram.

If you love deep sea free-diving, you can read the blogs from world champions. You can watch their movies in high definition, listen to their interviews, keep track of their adventures, and even buy the same gear that they use.

On the internet you aren't weird or fussy and you don't have strange taste. You are part of a "tribe," a gang of people who believe as you believe. This gang has conversations that "regular people" wouldn't understand.

This gang has leaders. The Key People of Influence are the ones who lead these small, powerful movements.

Never has there been more meaningful work that needs to be done. Never has there been a better time to make a difference on the planet. Never has there been a better time to position yourself as a Key Person of Influence.

THE SINGER AND THE MICROPHONE

Imagine we live in 1876 and the first microphone has just been invented. It's an exciting new device that takes the human voice and amplifies it to a greater audience. This new technology is fascinating to a lot of people. Imagine the seminars and courses on how to set up a microphone, how to switch it on, how to fiddle with the dials. Imagine people start writing articles like "How To Make Money With A Microphone," "Microphone Secrets," and "Microphone Wealth Creation."

To some people it seems like the microphone is making people rich, but they are missing the point. The money doesn't go to people who know how a microphone works, it goes to the people who know how to sing.

A bad singer just becomes a louder bad singer with a microphone in their hand.

The world is full of great tools now. YouTube offers you business video production tools, Facebook has tools for advertising and audience building, WebinarJam lets you host free on-demand webinars. These companies have all invested millions upon millions of dollars to create tools to help you run your business.

These tools are the modern-day "microphone."

Unfortunately, people get focused on the wrong thing…

INVEST IN ASSETS NOT TOOLS

The problem is, tools don't grow your business, assets do—and these tools don't work without you plugging your assets into them.

A YouTube account doesn't do much unless you upload an engaging video. Facebook Ads need compelling images, video, and copy. Webinars need you to have slides and a script that sells.

Assets are unique to your business.
Tools are available for everyone to use.

Struggling businesses obsess over tools. They put hours of research into understanding the features of a CRM system, they get excited about email automation software, they read blogs about shopping carts and which colour button had the highest click-through rate. They shell out thousands of dollars each month on these tools thinking they're going to get a massive return.

The truth is, although you will see a decent return (whether that's revenue or saving time), creating and using an asset is where you'll find the biggest return.

Successful businesses obsess over their assets—and I'm not just referring to their office buildings. They focus on capturing powerful stories on video, they write insightful content, they win awards for their work, and they get extremely specific about their company brand and culture.

Armed with great assets like books, reports, videos, and a honed message, these companies quickly discover that any of the tools they use come to life and perform. Their books sell well on Amazon, their videos on YouTube generate a big audience, their groups on Facebook have a dozen new members join every hour because people can see the unique points of difference.

A business with amazing assets can use very basic tools and get a huge result. Conversely, a business with every tool ever developed but nothing much to say is dead in the water.

We live in an era where tools will actually come and find you if your assets are good enough. Your job as an entrepreneur is to create assets first and then look for tools that can leverage them—not the other way around.

Your business will not suddenly change (certainly not long term) because you've discovered some tool developed by another company.

It doesn't really matter what CRM system you use, or if you have a robot tweeting 100 times a day on autopilot, or if you're subscribing to a webinar platform that has all the bells and whistles built right into its features.

When you have an ecosystem of assets, the tools suddenly become useful. Your business will take off when you have remarkable assets that are totally unique and can be leveraged across the multitudes of platforms (tools) that are available.

The good news is that you are probably a lot closer than you think to discovering valuable assets. Every business owner is sitting on assets, whether it's a particular way you do business, content that only lives within your head or a methodology you've built to bring success to your clients. Whatever it is, you need to be in the right environment to unpack your mind and create those assets.

KEY IDEAS

- The rules of the Industrial Revolution have changed.
- The world is now a deeply connected place and it requires a new type of leadership.
- People can find what they are looking for no matter where it is on the planet. They want it to be special, relevant, and trustworthy.
- Traditional big business typically can't cater to these specific requirements of trust, character, and uniqueness.
- Small highly niched businesses will emerge as very profitable and fun places to be contributing to.
- Every niche will require a face to represent it. This will create the need for hundreds of Key People of Influence in every industry.
- Technology is only valuable if you have a powerful message.
- To learn more about becoming the 'go-to' person in your niche, watch this short video from Mike: www.learnkpi.com

NOTES ...

NOW IS THE TIME TO BE A KEY PERSON OF INFLUENCE

We could not have written this book at any time in the past. Through the middle ages, you were either nobility or you were a serf. In the Industrial Revolution there were only two types of people: those who could afford a factory and those who could not. There would be no point in telling people to go after their dreams: they had no means of production through which to be vital; most people had to be functional or they would starve.

Today all that has changed. Every industry you can imagine can be broken down into micro-niches, and each one needs a Key Person of Influence.

When someone asks, "Who's the best wedding make-up artist in Majorca?" you can Google search and easily find out.

If someone wants to go on a vacation for Jewish singles they can find the person who organizes those. Crowd-funding for startup entrepreneurs? Someone's leading that conversation. A courier for stem cells? You'll find the person who's thought this through.

In the next ten years there will be huge advantages for people who stand out as Key People of Influence in their chosen field. Teams will form around them, people will track them down from around the world, and the top money will flow to those who step up as KPIs in their industry.

Fortunately, you are at the beginning of a trend. Things are possible today that were not possible just a few years ago. You are a "first settler" in a brave new world.

THE SETTLERS AND THE SWAGMEN

Both Daniel and Mike are Australian and were brought up hearing the stories about the "first settlers" of the 1800s.

At that time the agricultural-age rules applied, so in order to create wealth and power first settlers staked their claim to a piece of land. They settled in one place and then worked their land to produce as much as they could from it; this became the place where they built their fortune.

People who failed to claim a piece of land wandered around aimlessly, doing odd jobs for the people who owned the land. These itinerant workers were called "swagmen" because they carried all their possessions in rolled-up "swags" on their backs as they navigated from farm to farm. They had no place to call home and they just kept wandering around looking for any work they could find. After a while all the workable land was claimed and they were stuck feeling resentful that they hadn't staked their land when they had the chance. They complained that they worked hard and didn't get paid enough.

In this new intangible economy, the first settlers create wealth and power by staking their claim to a niche or a micro-niche.

Owning a micro-niche is as valuable as owning land. If you are known as a Key Person of Influence in your field, you will attract the money and the opportunities that are flowing around that niche. Even when you pass opportunities to others, your wealth and power grows.

Some people in the ideas economy aren't staking their claim to a niche or a micro-niche. They are the modern-day swagmen wandering around working on various projects but failing to claim their own niche. They keep coming up with new ideas but aren't brave enough to settle on something and really own it. They want to try and please everyone but they don't attract anyone.

After a while all the micro-niches in their industry will have Key People of Influence who have established themselves, and these wandering swagmen will wish they had claimed their place sooner.

They will resent the KPIs and say, "I could have done that," even though they didn't.

Do you want to be a swagman or a Key Person of Influence?

You can't have it both ways. You can't be a jack of all trades and a master of none. You can't be a Key Person of Influence at "all sorts of things." You have to pick something that you are going to become known for and you need to start promoting it and turning away anything that isn't quite right.

Now is the time to claim your piece of land. It's time to say:

I won't try to be all things to all people.
What I do is special and I have my own unique way of doing it.
Anything else isn't for me.

EVERY INDUSTRY WILL BE FINELY SLICED

In every industry there are going to be micro-niches within niches. Each micro-niche will be an opportunity for a Key Person of Influence to claim it as their space because the internet doesn't really help generalists to stand out.

HERE ARE SOME EXAMPLES OF NICHES AND MICRO-NICHES:

Niche: Health and Wellness
Micro-niches: Raw food parties, body-transformations for busy executives, fresh juice delivery, ten-day detoxing retreats, natural supplements in cakes, vegetarian marathons.

Niche: Small Business Services
Micro-niches: Hair salon marketing, Facebook advertising, testimonial video production, low-cost virtual assistants for estate agents.

Niche: House and Family

Micro-niches: Dog furniture, accelerated learning for babies, portraits of horse owners with their horses, custom-designed home cinemas.

Niche: Clothing and Apparel

Micro-niches: Fashion with motivational quotes, non-leather "leather" jackets, fashion advice for CEOs.

Niche: Travel and Lifestyle

Micro-niches: LGBT travel, cruises for over 65s, follow the F1 circuit for a year, scuba diving to rebuild a reef.

EXERCISES

- Make a list of possible micro-niches in the industry you most enjoy.
- Google some of these micro-niches to see if someone has already claimed this space or if it's still available for you to own (soon we will discuss how).

If there was one specific thing you would love to be known for, what would it be?

NOTES ...

YOU ALREADY HAVE A UNIQUE SET OF SKILLS AND TALENTS

The very good news is that in this "new found land," your greatest
assets are your existing passion, the skills you already have and, most
of all, your own personal story.

You may think that the key to your wealth lies in some mystical
wealth creation vehicle that you don't yet know about. Maybe you
think it's the stock market, property development, a franchise or
perhaps a new e-commerce website.

The truth is that your real wealth is in your story. Your journey
thus far has not been a waste of time; it's been perfect. Your hobbies
and interests are not meaningless, they are a gold mine. Your
passion isn't hollow; it's the best fuel you will ever have. You've
already been a leader within certain circles. You already have
examples of people you've helped, teams you've built, and value
you've added. You need to harness what you have and refine it.

I've seen people build fun, profitable lifestyle businesses from:

- Providing nightclubs with packaged marketing and
  promotions.
- Giving strategies for couples to get pregnant faster.
- Helping professional speakers fine tune the last ten
  minutes of their talks.
- Sourcing investment properties for young professionals
  who work for major banks or consulting firms.
- Giving financial advice to celebrities.
- Selling special bags of organic mixed fruit and nuts that
  replace all meals for a week.
- Helping art collectors to buy rare sculptures.

But here's the problem: every day on your news feed you will read a
story about an individual who has made big money doing some new
thing. The assumption you may wrongly make is that it was the

"thing" that made the money. You might think it was the product or the industry that was responsible for their success and miss that it was, in fact, the marriage of that "thing" with that person's story.

You may curse yourself for missing out on the latest trends:

"We should have been in the software business."

"Corporate training is really where the money is at."

"Oh, if only I were helping people buy, renovate, and sell property."

Their thing might not be *your* thing. What you may miss altogether is the story behind the story.

The person who just made a fortune from real estate loved looking at real estate deals long before they got rich doing it.

The person who works with big corporations spent twenty years in C-suite executive roles before they started their business.

The guy with the lucrative, organic fruit and nuts business has been writing about health and wellness issues since he was sixteen years old.

It's their story that people buy into. You like them. You like their take on things. You like their ideas. You see how connected and admired they are in their industry. You want to spend time and money with them because they are a Key Person of Influence and that's attractive to you. The person in the story hasn't found *the* thing, they have found *their* thing. However, I could almost guarantee that it's not *your* thing. Unless you have been keenly interested in something for several years, forget trying to be a success story in that field any time soon. You simply can't beat the people who genuinely love an industry, and not because they think it is a quick formula for cashing in.

There is already a theme to your life that has been unfolding. It may seem that you have done many things or that you have some strange and unrelated talents, but it hasn't been random at all. Everything you have done up until this point has been for a specific reason. It's been building up to this moment. It has brought you right here to this chapter in this book where you can get this message:

> *You are already standing on a mountain of value. Your story is valuable, your experience is unique, and you are highly valuable… just as you are!*

You don't need to learn new skills; you are ready to create value now. You are no longer on this planet to be a consumer; you are here to produce.

You're ready to establish yourself as a Key Person of Influence through creative output, not through further consumption. All of your future learnings will come from the process of producing value, not through pursuing other people's stories or chasing distant trends.

This may rattle you a little. Surely, if you were valuable already you would already be earning the serious money? No, the reason you don't have the money yet is that you have not established yourself as a KPI and you haven't crystallized your value. In the next few chapters you will see exactly how to do this in five clear steps.

When you are ready, let's take a look at the Key Person of Influence Method.

EXERCISES

- Map out the timeline of your life with high points and low points. Start out as early as you can remember and try to remember some of the details for each memory.
  Once you have your life's timeline, look for the themes.
- Make a list of your skills and talents and see if you can join them up to see the themes.

ACTIVITY

On your bathroom mirror stick a sign that reads:

"I am already standing on a mountain of value. My story is valuable, my experience is unique, and I am highly valuable as I am. All of my future learnings will come from the process of creative output."

NOTES ...

2

THE KEY PERSON OF INFLUENCE METHOD

A KPI traditionally refers to the term "Key Performance Indicator"—a benchmark that people measure themselves against. Likewise, a Key Person of Influence sets a standard that others aspire to. If you become a Key Person of Influence, people will associate you with the level of performance they want to align with.

It's time for you to become a KPI.

STEPPING INTO THE INNER CIRCLE

In every industry there's an inner circle of Key People of Influence. If there's a good opportunity in their industry these people are the first to be told. If they don't like the opportunity, they pass it to another KPI. If all the KPIs don't like the opportunity they kick it out to the outer circle.

This sets up an interesting situation. The inner circle is rich with good opportunities shared between a small number of people. The outer circle is full of many people fighting over the poorer opportunities. For this reason…

Until you are a Key Person of Influence in the industry you love,
your full-time job is to become one.
#kpimethod

Let's look at the stats in Canada—a country with a high degree of equality compared to other OECD nations. It turns out the top 20% of Canada's wealthy control half of Canada's entire wealth. And the wealthiest 5% of families control nearly 50% of that half alone.

The research says that over the last thirty years, since the information age came along, the top 10% of earners in almost every industry have grown their incomes by 300% while the majority have gone sideways or slipped backwards.

What does this tell you about how money works across Canada? It tells you that it's not even close to being "fairly" distributed. Wealth moves to and from a small percentage of Key People of Influence.

We're not here to tell you this is right or wrong. We understand that all sorts of problems arise from inequality. Our goal is to leave you better informed so you can choose whether you want to be in the top 10% or not. We will say, however, that your ability to have a positive impact on issues like inequality is far greater from that vantage point.

Even if you are in the top 20% of earners you can expect to be sharing in a high percentage of the wealth. If you aren't, you will be fighting it out with the other 80% of people for the smallest percentage of the wealth—it will be exhausting and dehumanizing.

It works in much the same way inside larger organizations too. The top 20% of companies in any industry often generate more than 80% of the revenue in that whole industry. The top 10% of people who run those top companies are earning more than ever, while the majority of people are trying to budget their monthly pay.

If you've heard about people taking an exponential leap in their earnings, let us shed some light on it.

If a person moves from about the average in their industry into the top third of earners, they won't actually see a big shift in their income or their influence. They won't really get any special treatment, they won't hear about fresh opportunities, and they won't stand out significantly in their industry even though they moved from the mid-point to the top third.

If that same person moves into the top 10% of their industry, their life changes dramatically.

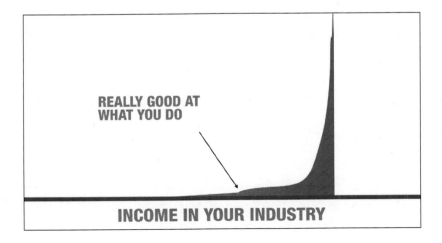

REALLY GOOD AT
WHAT YOU DO

INCOME IN YOUR INDUSTRY

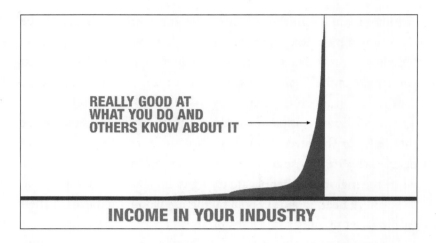

As soon as a person crosses into the inner circle of their industry, they start sharing the biggest slice of the pie with a small number of their new contemporaries.

As they progress deeper into the inner circle and establish themselves as a Key Person of Influence, their income takes a leap, they get invited into important meetings, their voice gets heard, and they have more input. It becomes a virtuous loop: the more input, the more they are seen as valuable and the more they get known as a Key Person of Influence in their field.

You must orchestrate your move into the inner circle of the industry you love; it's the most rewarding thing you can do. There's very little happening outside the inner circle that can reward you for what you're worth.

HOW ARE YOU SHOWING UP?

Since 2011 both Daniel and Mike have been building a training and advisory company called Dent Global.

We would regularly host events to teach people the KPI Method and hire sought-after leaders and entrepreneurs to mentor our clients through the twelve-month Key Person of Influence Accelerator program.

In that time, we've seen well over 10,000 businesspeople attend our events and would witness first-hand what held some of them back from succeeding and let others rise to the top 10%.

These environments are usually brimming with opportunities and a KPI can walk away with more business than they know what to do with.

Before any event even began, we would watch people meeting each other and what we saw was insightful.

Most people are abysmal at generating any attraction with others even in an environment that's bustling. Most people walk away from a high-quality business event with nothing more than a small stack of business cards from people who have no interest in doing any business with them.

It's crazy; they are at an event with hundreds of motivated, screened people and yet somehow they can't do any business as a result of being there.

It's not because they are bad people, or because they don't have any value to share. It's simply that they have never been taught how to represent themselves as a Key Person of Influence. They are often unclear about the value they can offer; they seem to lack credibility that others can gauge; they come across as burned-out, lacking enthusiasm or unwilling to do anything to win business.

A Key Person of Influence doesn't show up that way. They are clear, credible, and energized, and they don't seem needy. They have the groundwork in place so they can show up confidently.

It doesn't take long to see the difference. At almost every event we've hosted, someone will come up to us and ask to be a speaker at our next conference, be promoted to our database or do another sort of deal.

As Mike would say, "At this point, I don't care if they are a trained speaker or if they have a well-conceived deal in mind. First, I need to know if they are a Key Person of Influence."

So I ask some typical questions—some I ask directly and other things I'm mentally checking for:

QUESTION 1. WHAT DO YOU DO?

It seems like a very open and general question, but I actually want to know they can stand out purely on how they pitch themselves at this point.

Most people say their job title or profession: "I'm a management consultant," "I'm a dentist," "I run a car dealership," "I'm in recruitment."

Other people attempt to be unique and say something like "I motivate people to be their best," or something vague like "I help people get what they want," or general, along the lines of "I help businesses grow."

A KPI lights up when you ask them what they do. They are prepared and already know you'll be impressed with what they have to say. In under two minutes, they have you hooked. Their response has been honed and it's powerful. They speak clearly, with authority and relevance. They often communicate more in two minutes than others do in an hour.

QUESTION 2: WHAT MAKES YOU CREDIBLE?

Sometimes I'm mentally looking for clues, sometimes I might ask things like, "Do you have a book? Do you have a following? Are you published in any journals or magazines? Do you have any remarkable case studies? Do you have any unique insights that few people can articulate?"

If I do ask, most people fumble and feel awkward that they have no proof of their value. They say "I've been doing this for fourteen years" or "You should see my work."

A KPI will ooze credibility. They will tell you about their insights, their thought leadership, and the publications they are featured in. They will talk about their case studies and success stories; within seconds you know they are a legitimate professional in their field.

QUESTION 3: HOW DO YOU MAKE YOUR MONEY?

Maybe I'll ask directly or maybe I'm just fishing for answers: "Do you have a day rate? Do you have products? Do you broker someone else's products and services? What do people usually pay you and are they typically happy with it?"

Most of the time their "product" is them. They need to physically turn up in order to deliver value.

Conversely, they may have a product that is generic so I instantly compare it to other products in the market and I can't see what's special about their offering.

A Key Person of Influence has an elegant business model backing them up. They have an ecosystem of products and services that all fit nicely with their brand. They know how to differentiate their products just by the way they describe them.

QUESTION 4. ARE YOU KNOWN, LIKED, AND TRUSTED BY OTHERS?

Everyone has a history and I'm curious to know what happens if I Google your name. Are there blogs? Will great videos of you come up on YouTube? Will I see that you have thousands of social media followers? Will I find anything nasty? Will I find anything about you at all?

Most people don't have a profile even when you Google their name. If you're lucky you'll get their LinkedIn and Twitter accounts. Rarely will you see blogs, videos, podcasts, and community pages. It's even more unlikely that you'll find feature articles about them from external sources, reviews or interviews.

Many people want someone else to build their profile or expect they will get a profile after a deal comes off. The problem is that deals won't even get started if a person is an unknown commodity.

A KPI shows up when you Google them. They have several coherent social media profiles. You'll find engaging video and audio; you'll see them written up in traditional media; and you'll see their work reviewed by third parties.

QUESTION 5. WHO OR WHAT ELSE CAN YOU BRING TO THE DEAL?

I can bring a lot to a deal: money, contacts, distribution, products, celebrity endorsers. Apart from the obvious, I'm interested to know what else you bring to a deal. Do you bring with you access to new products, big brands, wide reaching distribution, celebrities, skilled team members, databases, or even money? Do you know how to structure a deal? Do you think win/win?

Often people will communicate inadvertently that they want the whole deal to be easy for them and difficult for us. They want to show up and speak, have our company promote their products or have us buy what they have to sell without asking too many questions.

When a KPI approaches us, doing a deal is easy, but their approach is win/win. They volunteer the additional benefits they bring to the deal. They have already thought about how the deal might be structured so it's almost risk free. They make sure they take on an equal share of the burden to execute the deal because they know how much work is actually involved in getting anything meaningful achieved.

Within minutes we know the difference between a Key Person of Influence and someone who's not there yet. It doesn't take long to do a deal or to pass on an opportunity because we know the KPI is prepared.

In the next chapters we're going to outline an explicit five-step method designed to address these important questions and ensure that you are seen to be a Key Person of Influence in your industry. It builds in clarity, credibility, scale, transparency, and commercial viability. It's designed to leverage your story, your experiences, your insights, and your personality.

When you're ready to learn and apply this method, read on.

BONUS

For an introduction to the five principles, you can watch this short video from Mike: www.learnkpi.com

THE KEY PERSON OF INFLUENCE METHOD

Across all industries, the top opportunities go directly to a small group who position themselves as Key People of Influence in that field. The rest of those in the industry are left to fight over the opportunities that the KPIs turn down. It might sound unfair, but that's how it is.

It's not that hard to become a Key Person of Influence and it certainly doesn't take years to achieve. There are just five things that you need to have in place to demonstrate that you are a Key Person of Influence:

1. Pitch—your ability to communicate your value and uniqueness through your spoken word.

Key People of Influence can answer the question "What do you do?" with power and clarity.

Powerful pitching is the ability to clearly communicate your message in a way that influences and enrols supporters into your projects.

Pitching is a vitally important skill. If you have something of great value to offer but no one can understand it, you're not going any further.

Throughout history, every great business, movement or cause began with a powerful pitch. Armed with little more than their words, many change-makers, leaders, and entrepreneurs have launched a business, recruited teams, gained funding, and even changed the world.

Conversely, many people who have had great ideas and personal resources couldn't get things done when their pitch was lousy.

Key People of Influence pitch for specifics. They don't cast a wide net; they are laser focused. Their pitch has gravitas.

When you have a great pitch you don't just make more money and attract great people, you also have more fun, attract further opportunities, and experience deeper rewards.

2. Publish—Your ability to gain credibility through authoring content.

Published content creates ownership and authority over your chosen niche or micro-niche. If we were in the agricultural age you'd need the Title Deed to your land. In a global market full of ideas, content published online shows ownership; it puts your name on your work. Published books, articles, and reports tell the world that you are an authority in your field. It's no coincidence that the word "authority" has the word "author" in it.

These days you can easily publish and print e-books; you can instantly upload blogs; it's inexpensive to make beautifully designed reports—and it's almost effortless to make it all available globally. If you publish, your ideas get seen and they spread faster.

The process of writing will make you smarter than most in your field: it will sharpen your communication skills, improve your ad copy, develop your stance on each topic, and help you to spot trends in your thinking. Published content on its own is an intellectual property asset that can be further developed in your products.

3. Product—Your ability to scale your value through an elegant product and services ecosystem.

Turning your skillset into an asset is an essential part of becoming a Key Person of Influence and this happens when you productize your intellectual property.

You must have several products, each designed to complement the overall mission you have as a Key Person of Influence. Part of that challenge is to have some products that are built for high volume and some that are built for high value.

Products help you to become known and transfer value. Even services businesses can create a "productized service" and develop additional products that complement the core services business.

As soon as you develop quality products you'll increase your opportunities to scale and even go global if you want to.

4. Profile—Your ability to become known, liked, and trusted in your industry.

When people do a search for your name, you must come up on the first results page in order to show you are clearly a Key Person of Influence in your chosen field.

There is no longer an excuse for being invisible online—you are who Google says you are. If you're invisible, you won't complete bigger deals no matter how well you pitch.

You're in control of your online profile. It's your responsibility to create a powerful online presence using social media and traditional media hand in hand.

It's important to clean up anything that's confusing or outdated and to remove anything that doesn't serve your personal brand.

With a well-crafted profile you'll find that perfect inbound opportunities start to show up regularly and you get more success with what you go after.

5. Partnership—The ability to structure and maintain strategic relationships that benefit everyone involved.

As you may have guessed, the real wealth comes when you complete this final stage and begin leveraging with others in an effective way.

The spirit of partnership generates a multiplier effect. Rather than two people competing over how to slice a pie, they work together to build a bakery and produce more pies than they know what to do with.

Consider that there is already someone who has a list of thousands of potential customers for your product; that there are already experts in your industry who would jump at the chance to be interviewed by you to create a product that enhances their brand and yours; that there are already people who have products that your contacts would be interested in and they would happily pay you a healthy percentage for making the sale.

WATCH THE RESULTS COME

When you have all five steps in place, you will be amazed at what happens to your life. You will be asked to speak at events, you will be referred to as an "expert," you will get more focused opportunities coming your way, you will be able to access most people in your industry and you will earn more money with less struggle.

I've watched this method transform people's lives and businesses in fifty different industries in a dozen different countries. If you implement this method, it will transform your business and your life too.

This isn't "voodoo" and it's not a gimmick; this method is based on best practices you can regularly see working in the real world. These five strengths are the cornerstones of hyper-resourceful people. You will become a person of vitality rather than a person of functionality if you implement this method.

Sadly, you get no points for trying to complete these steps. You only see big results after all five steps are completed to a high standard. Almost having a book means you have zero books on Amazon. Almost having a product means you have nothing to sell but your time. Almost doing a partnership means you are still working alone.

For some time you'll be putting in the effort and the results won't appear because the five steps aren't yet complete. Stay with it, keep going—it will be worth it when you've completed all the steps. Influence comes from output, not from hard work.

In the next chapters we will examine ways to get a breakthrough in each of the five steps of the KPI Method.

KEY PERSON OF INFLUENCE SCORECARD

What gets measured gets improved. We've devised a tool to measure your industry influence so you can focus on areas that need the most improvement.

Before you read on, answer the Key Person of Influence Scorecard questions at: www.scalemyinfluence.com

This set of questions is designed to score you on the five areas of influence described in this book. It gives you a customized report based on your answers.

The results of this scorecard will give you a starting point and show you where you are already strong and where you need to focus your attention.

17% COMPLETED

IF SOMEONE GOOGLED YOUR NAME, WOULD THEY FIND MOST OF PAGE 1 IS POSITIVE LINKS FEATURING YOU?

YES NO

STEP 1: PITCH

Your "perfect pitch" is so much more than you think. The truth is, with a perfect pitch you will be swamped with opportunities.

Many of the greatest wealth-creators and change-makers throughout history started with little more than a persuasive pitch.

Here are some excerpts from perfect pitches that changed the world:

> *"I have a dream that someday this nation will live up to its creed that all men are created equal."*
> **Dr Martin Luther King Jr**

> *"We choose to go to the moon by the end of this decade, not because it's easy but because it's hard."*
> **John Fitzgerald Kennedy**

> *"Let's measure the success of corporations by how much they enhance human well-being."*
> **Anita Roddick**

> *"You must be the change you want to see in the world."*
> **Mahatma Gandhi**

Can you imagine asking these visionaries, "What do you do?"

Their response would be so exhilarating, provocative, and contagious that you would want to help them in any way you could. That is how you want people to react to your ideas too.

I often ask businesspeople to rate themselves on how well they think they answer the question "What do you do?"

Most give themselves seven or eight out of ten—but does this reflect the true potential of a great pitch?

Consider that everyone you meet knows 150 people fairly well. A ten out of ten would mean they want to tell everyone about you. They would want to phone their most prized contacts and introduce you. A ten out of ten means that people might update their Facebook status about you, give their time to your cause, and share resources with you.

With this in mind, most people rate poorly for their pitching skills. They let too many opportunities go to waste in every interaction.

Don't be discouraged; get excited. There is massive room to grow just by improving the way you describe what you are up to in the world.

After you get this right, when someone asks you the quintessential networking question "What do you do?" your answer will have the power to unlock resources.

A not-so-potent answer will elicit a polite response, but nothing much will come of the interaction. We need to tune in to the real response you're getting.

BEWARE OF THE POLITE RESPONSE

A polite comment is one of the worst responses you can get when you tell people what you do. It is polite responses that keep you looking good but going nowhere. You can go nowhere for years because of polite responses.

Most people think it is encouraging that others nod and smile. When someone says "Sounds interesting" or "How long have you been doing that?" it is actually a meaningless non-response. They are being polite, but in truth are not engaged or interested.

What you want is an emotionally-charged response. They should either love it or hate it. Ideally, you want to see some immediate action.

You want people to engage with you. They should either want to pull out their calendar and make a time to talk to you, open their contacts and put you in touch with someone they know, or tell you "Your idea will never work!"

Positive or negative, a strong reaction is much better than a polite, benign response because you know they are listening and considering your ideas, not dismissing you. You must stir up a reaction and make a connection—be anything but boring.

A REAL PITCH GATHERS PACE

It isn't just for one-to-one interactions that your perfect pitch comes out to play. The day you get invited to speak in front of a group or to the media is the day your life can change dramatically.

Perfecting your pitch leads to bigger audiences and faster results each time it's delivered.

Clients we've worked with often start out with an average pitch. Within days of crafting a better pitch they see people responding differently to them and they often win unexpected business. A year later, if they have consistently pitched more powerfully they find themselves in the media and on stage.

I have seen a forty-five-minute talk raise millions; I have seen an eight-minute pitch that resulted in over 250 people rushing to grab a business card from the presenter (it held up the event by over thirty minutes); I've watched eighteen-minute talks that have changed my outlook on life.

When you know "what you are up to in the world" you become a magnet for opportunity. When you can communicate that message to a group, you speed up time and can achieve a month's work in a day.

But who are you to command that attention? Who are you to have people rushing your way? What's so special about you? Let's find out.

YOU ARE ALREADY STANDING ON A MOUNTAIN OF VALUE

Remember, your story is already more valuable than you think. Don't dare throw out your history. Sometimes it is simply that it is difficult to see your own value and you need to speak with others about your ideas and dreams to clarify or simplify it.

Part of the reason I moved to Canada was because I've always loved the wilderness and the mountains. I've climbed many of the highest peaks all over the world, and each time I do the same thing occurs to me. From the summit you get a view of how massive all the smaller mountains are, and all of a sudden it doesn't feel like you are standing on one of the tallest mountains in the group. From that lofty vantage point, the peaks are equalized.

Similarly, most people are already standing on a mountain of value; however, it is difficult to see the size, shape, and attributes of your mountain when you are on it. When you look down at where you stand, all you see is the dirt beneath your feet; and when you look up, you see how impressive the other mountains are.

It is very easy to see value from a distance; you see the value in others so effortlessly, but you sometimes fail to notice the immense value in yourself.

This is why you need to engage with objective people you don't already know and get their input. You need to get someone else to reflect back to you what they see as your value and how it should be packaged.

We've run pitching workshops all over the world and seen that an experienced entrepreneur with some perspective can often tell you more about the value you offer than your closest friend or spouse.

Get yourself around a dynamic person or group who can take you through a process of questioning and making suggestions until you have a pitch that you feel proud of.

People who have worked with our team discover that their story is already of amazing value when pitched correctly. One of the most exhilarating things I get to witness on a regular basis is when someone breaks through and sees how much they have to offer the world just as they are.

Sometimes it is overwhelming to people when they see what they have been hiding. It's like discovering you have an original Van Gogh sitting in your basement! Right under your nose is a mountain of value. Many people unlock a burst of energy they never knew they had when they start to sense it.

IMPOSTER SYNDROME IS PART OF ENTREPRENEURSHIP

I don't know any great entrepreneur who doesn't experience self-doubt on some level. That's because if you're up to something in the world then you are usually pushing the edge of your comfort zone to achieve it.

As you pitch your ideas and take on bigger and bigger projects, it's normal to ask questions like: Who am I to do this? Can I really pull it off? What if I get "found out" for not being qualified to do this? After all, you are growing, and all growth happens at the border between chaos and order.

Bear in mind that a business exists to take on the complexity and disorder of its clients. Taking on your clients' problems is why you are valuable to them in the first place. As you take on more complexity, chaos, and disorder in your business, you simultaneously experience more discomfort.

Discomfort is the precursor to progress. In fact, it's necessary to avoid being stuck in the status quo.

Key People of Influence aren't afraid to share their ideas with the world, knowing some people may disagree or even say negative things about them. In fact, they seek that out—it's how they know their ideas are hitting the mark!

They boldly take on projects or jobs that are out of their comfort zone or current capability—stretching is how they got to where they are in the first place. Sure, it requires them to backfill on their promises, but they believe in their ability to find a solution and deliver a great outcome. If the fear of being "exposed" for not having all the answers stopped them, they would never have achieved their current success.

We have a client in Sydney who runs a very successful payroll company. In addition to running a seven-figure business, she was asked to consult to one of the big four accounting firms in Australia. (Incidentally, she later got an eight-figure offer from this firm to buy her business—an offer that she turned down.) She says even she felt like an imposter when she first got offered the job.

Remember, you're already standing on a mountain of value. No matter what scale you're at, imposter syndrome is a normal part of growth. Embrace it as a sign you're on track and ready to take the next step in becoming a KPI.

DISCOVER YOUR "BIG GAME"

One of our mentors is a man who has built three multi-billion-dollar businesses. He has personally secured hundreds of millions' worth of investment for his ideas. He knows how to create a powerful pitch.

He says that at the heart of a perfect pitch is a mission, which he calls "Your Big Game"; it's what you want to be known for.

Your perfect pitch must contain your "why." It's your compass. It's the reason you get up each day.

Bill Gates said Microsoft's big game was "To put a personal computer in every home and on every desk in the world."

Ray Kroc said that McDonalds' big game was "If Man goes to the moon, we will go there too, open a restaurant and serve him a great burger at a great price."

Oprah Winfrey said her big game was to "Share a daily dose of inspiration with women all over the world."

Our big game is to "Create influential leaders and entrepreneurs all over the world who solve meaningful problems."

Your big game should:

- Get you out of bed raring to go in the morning and keep you up late at night.
- Become the heart of how you design your business and how you get results.
- Become the source of the irresistibly delightful experience you deliver to everyone who comes into contact with you.

Your perfect pitch is not just a set of well-rehearsed words. It is a statement about what you are up to in the world. It's your big game that lights you up just thinking about it.

THE COMPONENTS OF A GAME WORTH PLAYING

It must be fun: There is no point playing a game that is no fun. Sure it will have its struggles, challenges, and late nights, but it will still be an exciting and fun game you want to get up each day and play.

It must have rules: There are clear structures, time frames, and behaviour that is "out of bounds." You must be able to explain to people "the rules of the game." Someone on your team might ask, "Why do we spend so much time with customers after they already buy from us?" To which you might say, "One of the rules for the game is that we must have customers who feel respected and appreciated by us and rate us at least eight out of ten on customer service."

There must be players: Every game has players who come to the game because they consider their strengths are well suited for it.

The better your players, the more fun the game. It's fun to watch the NBA because all the players are almost superhuman. You want to create a game that attracts top players.

There must be a prize: Committed players love to play for the fun of the game, but when you have a coveted prize at stake everything goes to the next level. Is it money? Is it ownership? Is it recognition? Is it something even bigger? Whatever it is, the prize must be exciting for the players.

There must be a way to win: Imagine a game that has no end time. Imagine a game that doesn't keep score. Imagine a game where there is no clear way to win. It would not be fun and it would not keep people interested.

You get to set the goalposts and define what it means to win. Just like professional sporting events, your game should offer short-term wins as well as an overall championship victory. The thought of winning should stir you up emotionally and make you feel a surge of energy and focus.

There must be a way to lose: If you can't lose the game, then it's no fun either. The game must be edgy enough that the players realize it's entirely possible to lose.

The thought of losing the game should be a strong driver, and there should be a point where it is clear the game has been lost so players know when it's time to go back to the locker room and rethink their strategy.

The question you must ponder again and again is this:

> *"What's the big game I would love to play over the next three years—win or lose?"*

The answer needs to make you feel enlivened. When you have that answer you are ready to construct your pitch around your big game.

EXERCISES

- Write the words "My Big Game" in the centre of a piece of paper and mind map the factors that are important to you.
- Make sure you have insights for each of the six elements in your big game.

NOTES ...

YOU CAN'T PLEASE EVERYONE

Next you must choose your starting place for your big game to begin. This is the specific micro-niche you will tackle first.

Even a massive phenomenon like Facebook started out exclusively for Harvard University students to share their drunken photos; they then expanded to allow all university students. From a tiny micro-niche, big things can grow, but it almost never happens that a business sets out to please everyone and actually achieves it.

We've advised clients to get specific about their micro-niche and they resisted at first. It feels safer to stay open, general, and non-specific. Although it's counter-intuitive at first, we've seen time and time again our clients gain traction when they pitch their micro-niche.

Consider your niche and add more criteria. You need to know exactly who you are trying to serve or the problem you're out to solve. Your pitch might focus on a gender, an age group, a geography, an ideology or a socio-economic group. Sometimes it's based upon your best-ever client case study.

Your micro-niche should consist of people who you would enjoy connecting with and people who would equally enjoy connecting with you. If you are not a vegetarian, don't make it part of your niche just because you think it makes business sense. You will either get found out as a hypocritical meat-eater, or you will end up hating your business because it's not a good fit with who you are.

Choose a micro-niche that you identify with personally, with genuine concern and interest. You'll need to feel comfortable saying "no" to other opportunities until you've achieved a level of notoriety within this micro-niche. Choose carefully.

USE A SNIPER RIFLE, NOT A SHOTGUN

Intuitively, people believe that taking a general, all-encompassing approach to pitching is more effective than a narrowly focused pitch; experience shows me it is not. When you try to catch everyone in your net, you catch no one.

A broad approach is especially ineffective when your brand presence is weak. You need to become a laser-sharp marksman focusing on a very specific micro-niche.

For thousands of years people only did business with those who were geographically close to them. They bought from the baker down the road and the accountant nearby and went to their local toy store. In a world where geography was a natural barrier, a "general store" approach worked well because you could capture as many people as possible in your local vicinity.

Today we live in a world unlimited by geography. We are connected to each other with the swipe of a finger on a smart phone. People now buy from the companies they find when searching on their iPad, regardless of where the business is geographically located.

For this reason, you need to focus. You need to become known for the micro-niche and be prepared to sell to people wherever they are. The "general store" is now Amazon and you're not going to beat them at their game. Instead you'll use their technology to reach people all over the world.

Your micro-niche is something you pitch for. Whenever you are asked, "What do you do?" you share exactly the type of thing you are aiming for even though it can exclude other opportunities.

No more giving boring, general answers; from now on, go directly after the perfect client or project you want to work with.

WHAT IF YOU ARE IN A "BORING" INDUSTRY?

Remember the lady I mentioned who runs the payroll company in Sydney? When I met her, one of the first things she said to me was: "Mike, my business is boring. You can't make it sexy."

It's true, she wasn't flying rockets into space or teaching millennials how to trade cryptocurrency. She sold payroll services to large corporates.

Yet when I probed, it turned out she actually delivered massive cost savings and efficiency improvements into her client's companies. In some cases, she could save them hundreds of thousands of dollars in the space of a few months.

The more I probed, the more enthusiastic she got. She started talking about how antiquated some of their systems were and what kind of payroll technology was coming onto the market to massively reduce payroll complexity in large companies.

However, when she talked about these things, I could tell she took her expertise and knowledge for granted. She dismissed the valuable role her company played and downplayed their contribution. She was clearly very intelligent but just considered the work she did to be pretty beige and run-of-the-mill.

As we worked together to help her unpack her value through the Key Person of Influence Accelerator, we soon realized there was actually a big shake-up via new technology going on in her industry. She ended up writing a book called *Payroll Revolution* and a year later her second book called *Profit from Payroll*.

What happened next shocked her. She started being asked for her opinions in newspapers and online. She got invited to speak at conferences. She even decided to run one herself. Pretty soon she was flooded with more and more enquiries.

In an industry where very few people were stepping up as KPIs, she stood out by a country mile. It turns out what she considered boring was actually really interesting to her target market.

Remember, if you consider your field or industry boring its ripe for you and other KPIs to step up to the plate.

This is a golden opportunity. Don't leave it too late…

CONSTRUCTING A SOCIAL PITCH

You have a big game. You have a starting point. Now we need to address that age-old question "What do you do?" Your response can lead to a deep conversation or it can lead to polite (but disengaged) chit-chat. Your goal is to prepare a short answer to this question that lights people up and has them asking for more.

This social pitch gets used daily. It will end up being used online and others might even start using it when they introduce you. If you have a team, they need training to prepare a social pitch too.

Let's take a look at ten examples of how a normal response to the question "What do you do?" could be turned into a social pitch:

- **From:** "I have a PR agency. We do work on brand endorsement deals."
- **To:** "I run a PR agency. We specialize in matching celebrities with product endorsement deals. These deals make money for everyone involved and last for years. We've done deals for big businesses right through to startups."

- **From:** "I'm an M&A consultant. I help businesses grow through acquisitions."
- **To:** "I specialize in mergers and acquisitions. I help companies to buy out a competitor without using any cash. Many of my clients have doubled their revenue in a single deal."

- **From:** "I have a Financial Services business that provides advice."
- **To:** "I have a financial advice team who solve billion-dollar problems for governments and banks. We have fifty finance geniuses on our team who do nothing but crunch data on investments and risk. Our mission is to solve the financial crisis facing retiring baby boomers."

- **From:** "I have a training company that deals with HR issues."
- **To:** "I have a training company that teaches managers how to fire an employee properly. We are experts in how to have difficult conversations and to how to fire people so that they feel ok about it. We also save our clients a fortune in legal claims."

- **From:** "I design websites, blogs, and e-commerce platforms."
- **To:** "My design agency creates blogs for non-fiction authors. We help turn a book into a business. Typically our work results in more paid speaking, consulting, and book sales."

- **From:** "I'm a personal fitness instructor and I help people to lose weight or tone up."
- **To:** "I'm a fitness instructor. I take people on ten-day fitness retreats to Thailand to learn Thai-Boxing on the beach."

- **From:** "I'm a chartered accountant, but don't hold that against me!"
- **To:** "I'm a chartered accountant, I only work with consultants who charge over $500 a day. If a consultant is earning over $70,000 annually I can usually save them at least $3000 and two hours a week."

- **From:** "I make furniture and other goods."
- **To:** "I create rare, exclusive, one-of-a-kind boardroom tables and desks. Our tables and desks often go up in value and are collected by billionaires and celebrities. Recently we were appointed to supply our work to one of the world's most exclusive brands."

- **From:** "My wife and I are starting up a business doing travel related services."
- **To:** "I used to work for a major airline rewards program. I switched sides and now I help business owners game the system and fly around the world in business class for free on their points."

- **From:** "We shoot video for businesses. We can do anything relating to film production, editing, animation… stuff like that."
- **To:** "We film orientation and training videos that get shown to new members of staff in their first week. The goal is to get everyone representing the company properly from day one and create a high-performance culture."

WHAT DID YOU NOTICE?

These ten examples are based on real-life businesses we've worked with at Dent. As a result of improving that basic first response to the question "What do you do," they have generated a lot of business and opportunities in the real world, and they are more engaging than most people you'll meet.

In these examples the response focused on the value for the person listening versus the facts about the person speaking.

How will you change your social pitch?

BUILDING A STRONG PRESENTATION PITCH

Once people are hooked by what you do, they will want more. The goal is to make a scheduled time to deliver a "presentation pitch." This could range from a few minutes to a few hours, depending on the circumstances.

A presentation pitch can't be left to chance. When you have a captive audience you must be prepared to cover your bases. You also can't sound ill-prepared. You must know your pitch so well that it comes from your heart more than your memory. This means you need to write out a presentation pitch, learn it, and practise it until you own it.

You know you have it when you can talk passionately about your topic for three minutes or three hours without much preparation. Getting to this point requires you to start with some structure.

Let's take a look at some key things you need to know about your pitch.

YOUR PITCH CENTRES AROUND SOLVING A PROBLEM

People don't buy anything unless it solves a problem. They might not describe it that way; they might say they have a need, a want or a desire. The deeper truth is they only buy things that fix an underlying problem.

There is no value in coming up with an idea that doesn't solve a problem in a better way than is currently available. There's no point pitching an idea unless you understand what the problem is that you're able to resolve.

There are two types of problems to which the solutions are particularly valuable:

- Something people or businesses are already doing/buying which you can provide better, cheaper, more conveniently or with more emotional benefit.

- An unsolved problem people or businesses have, or will
  have soon, as a consequence of technological, economic,
  political, or social change, which you can predict and
  solve.

A PITCH MUST BE GROUNDED IN REALITY

For your pitch to have real power and value for others, they need
to see your idea is inspired by a genuine insight that is based in
reality. This means they want to know how you arrived at the ideas
in your pitch as well.

Ideas based on reality are almost always born from one of three
insights:

- **A Customer Insight.** One day you might have been
  shopping for something, and you just couldn't find what
  you were after, the service you received was terrible, you
  discovered something shocking—or you just knew that it
  could be done in a much better way. So you set out on a
  mission to right all the wrongs that you saw as a customer.
- **A Technology Insight.** You've spotted a way to use or create
  technology that solves a real problem or offers a brand-
  new benefit to people. You see that there's some new
  opportunity to combine your niche with a new technology
  and make life easier. Usually you're well experienced in
  this technology and you've spotted a new application for
  it.
- **An Industry Insight.** You know your niche so well that
  you've been able to figure out how things should be done
  better, faster, cheaper, more consistently, or with more fun.
  You've got deep insights into the future and you're going
  to be the first person there.

YOUR PITCH MUST BE ALIGNED TO YOUR STORY

When people hear you deliver your presentation pitch it must tell them more than just why this is a good idea; it must tell them why it's a good idea for you. For any idea to hold your attention long enough and gain traction, it must be aligned with your strongly held beliefs or else you will get bored with it.

A great presentation pitch leaves people with the feeling that you were "born to do this."

For Daniel and Mike, one of our own strong beliefs is that entrepreneurs and leaders can solve meaningful problems in an expansive way. We want to see a world where more people are empowered to be entrepreneurs and leaders.

This lines up with our personal story. From a young age, we've been using the entrepreneurial mindset to solve meaningful problems.

If we get involved in any business that is aligned to that mission, we know we will stay energized. Whenever either of us have tried to go after a good idea that didn't really line up with our values, it typically fizzled into an expensive learning experience.

QUICK EXERCISE

What strongly held belief do you have that makes you perfect for your business or idea?

I strongly believe…

YOUR PITCH MUST ARTICULATE THE PAYOFF

Your presentation pitch must articulate the benefits you bring to the person listening. Too many people talk about what they do, what they are good at, what they are experienced in or what they are qualified for. All of that is irrelevant if you don't translate it into a payoff for the person who's listening.

A dentist should talk about creating the perfect smile, removing people from pain or extending the life of youthful, clean teeth.

Lawyers should talk about protecting a business from a well-funded competitor, preventing an idiot from winning a spurious claim or ensuring the co-founders of a startup are energized and focused on the business rather than bickering over their percentages.

I recommend you have three core benefits that others will experience as a result of working with you.

For example, when I explain the Key Person of Influence Method I expand on the three big payoffs:

- You get to earn more money with less struggle.
- You get more recognition within the industry you love.
- You get to attract more of the right opportunities that energize you.

If people understand the payoff, they are interested in how to get it. Even if you have an amazing product, people won't buy from you if they can't figure out what it means to their life.

It's best to link your product to the classic, highly valued payoffs —more money, more time, better quality of life. Be as specific as you can.

QUICK EXERCISE

What three payoffs do you want to give to others?

HOW WILL YOU DELIVER THE RESULT?

Once we know *why* you want to do something and *what* it will do for others, the big question most people want answered next is *how* you will deliver it.

Will this be a consumable product? Will it be a service? Will it come as a subscription? Is it a training program? Is it an e-commerce shop? Will it be a retail store? How you get your value to others can be in many forms and it may grow over time.

Richard Branson has a big why: "to shake up old industries and give customers a more delightful experience." Virgin delivers three main promises: to give customers a better deal; to make its service fun; and to champion the needs of customers. How they deliver it is through trains, planes, credit cards, phones, festivals… and about 150 other businesses.

QUICK EXERCISE

How do you get these three valuable promises over to others?

CONSTRUCTING YOUR PRESENTATION PITCH

When you know the foundations of your pitch, life and business get easier. With strong foundations in place you can easily give a talk, write a brochure, create a new product, author a book, record a video or do a deal.

The most important next step is using these foundations in a nice logical order to share your ideas with others in a way that allows them to get enrolled in your vision.

There are many ways to structure a pitch. The first method I teach people when they are new to pitching is fairly basic.

POSITION YOURSELF AS CLEAR AND CREDIBLE:

It's clear to your audience who you are and why you are worth listening to. You might state something that reinforces this yourself, you might be introduced by a respected friend, you might arrive in your private jet (as any billionaire will tell you, the real value of a private jet isn't the leg room).

ARTICULATE THE PROBLEM AND HOW YOU NOTICED IT:

You have seen a real problem and you are calling attention to it. Richard Branson tells the story about how he was stranded in an airport and wondered if there was a better way to run an airline.

EXTRAPOLATE ON THE IMPACT OF THE PROBLEM:

You know that this problem impacts more areas of life than one might first think. You project forward into the future and stipulate what can arise if this problem isn't dealt with.

SOLVE IT:

Suggest that you have a way of solving this problem and share your ideas freely. Educate people on the key insight you have for making sure this problem is solved properly.

PROVE IT:

Back up your claim with some proof that it's a good idea; if you haven't got proof you can have a highly respected person vouch for what you are saying. Quote some statistics if you can or share a case study that adds weight to what you're saying.

To check out over 100 video case studies of people who have applied the KPI Method and positioned themselves as Key People of Influence in their industries, head to: www.dent.community

ASK FOR WHAT YOU WANT:

Finally, get them to share what you want in order to take the idea forward. Be specific, be bold, and be clear about what you want and why.

LEAVE PEOPLE UPLIFTED:

Don't finish a pitch on a flat note. You want to finish with a story, an idea or a vision for the future that gets people excited. People don't often remember everything you said but they surely remember the way you left them feeling. Be sure to deliberately leave people feeling something positive.

Use this structure to write out a pitch and rehearse it. It might seem a little too structured at first; however, with practice you will develop so much clarity in your own mind that you will be able to talk about your idea naturally and still hit these bases in the right order.

If your pitch sounds too rehearsed, you haven't rehearsed it enough.

PITCHING BONUS: PUBLIC SPEAKING AND MEDIA APPEARANCES

One of the fastest and most powerful ways to become a Key Person of Influence is to speak to groups, either at live events or through the media.

As a speaker or media personality, you are instantly transformed into an authority on your topic and you reduce the time it takes to get your message out.

One of the essential things all Key People of Influence must do is get comfortable giving their pitch to a group. This will only happen if you've practised your pitch one-on-one with hundreds of people.

The more you give your pitch to the people around you, the more likely it is that you'll be given an opportunity to leverage your message. It's virtually impossible to make it into the media or onto the stage if you can't deliver a powerful pitch to an individual first.

If the thought of public speaking or being featured in the media scares you, consider enrolling on a speaking course or working with a professional to ensure you can get your message across to a group as powerfully as you can do it in a one-to-one meeting. No one is born with speaking skills; the insider secret is that every great pitcher, speaker or media personality has had training.

Organize your pitch into a talk, and ready yourself for the day you get invited to take the stage or appear in the media. It will also help you in Steps 3 and 4 of the KPI Method when you go to create a product and an online presence.

EMBRACE THE CRITICS

A big fear people have when pitching their idea is getting what they perceive to be a negative response.

One of our mentors has raised hundreds of millions of dollars for his businesses. He tells us all the time that one of the best responses you can get when you tell someone your idea, is "That won't work!"

Rather than getting offended, he sees this negative reaction as an excellent opportunity to find out what people think is currently blocking the way forward.

If someone says to you, "That won't work," don't be offended; get curious. Ask them why they think it won't work. Be patient, ask lots of questions and write down the answers. It's these valuable insights that will draw you to discover the most important elements of your pitch that you need to get across.

If someone says that it won't work because "You won't find good staff who can deliver the specialized service," then your next pitch will become even more powerful when you say, "A big reason this hasn't been done before is because it's almost impossible to find the staff needed to deliver the service. We have been able to overcome that issue, and here's how…"

A typical startup entrepreneur wants people to love their ideas and hates it when someone points out even minor flaws in their plan. A more experienced leader realizes that a critical eye is a valuable thing and any shortcomings must be addressed in order to improve the plan.

Embrace the critics; they can be the source of your best insights.

A PERFECT PITCH POWERS PERFORMANCE

Your pitch is your foundation. It's the most basic asset you have as an entrepreneur, leader or change-maker; it's also one of your most powerful.

Larger companies, too, benefit when every person knows how to pitch. One of our clients taught his fifty-plus team how to pitch properly. Everyone, from the receptionist to the directors, had to know the three-minute pitch by heart. The results were stunning:

the entire company saw greater alignment, more energy, more innovation, and more sales, which could all be tracked back to this pitching activity.

Your pitch also forms the basis of the next steps in the KPI Method. From a great pitch you will be able to publish powerful content, develop hot products, build a trusted profile, and get others involved through partnerships.

Without a perfect pitch you should be cautious completing the next steps in this book (go ahead and read on, but be sure the first thing you do is to get your pitch right).

If your pitch has flaws they will show up in everything else you produce. A poor pitch will yield a boring book, products that are impossible to sell, websites that don't keep people reading, and fruitless partnerships.

You want to be sure that what you have to say is valuable, that you are excited by it, and that others can get excited too (or easily see it's not for them).

If you're happy with what you have created then get ready for the next step in the KPI Method.

You are about to see how to get an express pass to the inner circle of your industry by writing and publishing your ideas.

BONUS

If you would like to learn how to communicate your value so you can win more business, we developed a very powerful tool called the CAPSTONE Pitch Canvas. The Canvas provides an 8-step pitching framework that will help you clarify your value, generate more leads, and close a lot more business as a result.

You can download a copy of the Canvas here: www.pitchtheprize.com

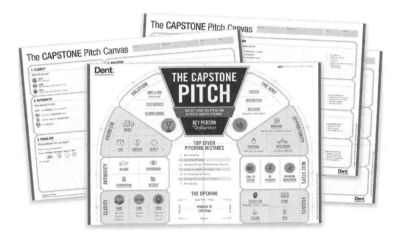

Throughout the remainder of the book you will see case studies of Canadian entrepreneurs who have built their brands as visible and respected leaders within their industry. While we have chosen to highlight these 'Key People of Influence' in this book (with their permission), we have not worked with them directly through the Dent Accelerators.

CASE STUDY: NICOLE VERKINDT, FOUNDER OF OMX

Nicole Verkindt is the founder of OMX (theomx.com), a B2B online procurement platform connecting local contractors and suppliers with large domestic and international procurement opportunities in the defence, aerospace, oil and gas, mining, and infrastructure industries, and in public sectors.

What does that all mean? Well, for example, when a large multinational company wins a contract with the Canadian government (in, say, aerospace or defence), by law they must "offset" that money leaving Canadian borders by purchasing domestic products and services from local Canadian suppliers.

If that sounds complicated to communicate, don't worry, you're not alone. This isn't an easy business to explain in lay terms. Yet, today, OMX is the number-one procurement platform in its niche, with over 150,000 suppliers and 130,000 opportunities across 189 countries.

How did Nicole build OMX into such a fast-growing and dominant player in her field? Well, as Rob Segal—one of her investors and the former CEO of Virgin Gaming, the online tournament gaming division of Richard Branson's Virgin Group—said, "[OMX is a] can't-say-no proposition, with better product, better pricing, and better service."

Key People of Influence recognize building a remarkable product within a micro-niche (like a government offset procurement marketplace for complex supply chains), carries a serious advantage. It's cheaper and easier to become the obvious "go-to" choice for what you do.

Nicole grew up in the aerospace industry, with her parents running a business that supplied high-tech products to large aerospace companies in Canada. Her domain knowledge working in her parents' business perfectly positioned her to later start OMX.

Nicole hasn't simply relied on having the "best technology" or product alone to fuel the success of OMX. While her product has evolved from its earliest iterations into a far more comprehensive solution, she understood that a powerful product is only as good as a powerful pitch. Whether it was pitching for investors, key stakeholders or partners, Nicole refined her pitch over and over until she could distill the value of OMX into a clear and coherent answer to the question "What do you do?"

Nicole has also been very active in sharing her unique insights and knowledge in as many forums as possible to drive awareness of both her personal brand and the company brand as well. When you Google "Nicole Verkindt" you will see she dominates the first page with feature articles in the likes of the *Toronto Star*, the *Globe and Mail,* and the *Financial Post*, as well as being a columnist for Vanguard Canada, to name a few.

As a result of her business success, she's been actively recognized for numerous awards such as StartUp Canada's 2019 Woman Entrepreneur Ambassador of the year, StartUp Canada's 2017 Woman Entrepreneur of the Year and Adweek's 2018 "Toronto Brand Stars." She also featured as a Dragon on CBC's *Next Gen Den* and is an investor in early-stage tech companies on Gimlet Media's *The Pitch*. In addition, she is a regular commentator on CBC News and BNN.

Nicole sits on numerous boards of organizations including the Canadian Crown Corporation, the Canadian Commercial Corporation, and the Canadian Chamber of Commerce. She is also a Next Gen member of the Canadian Business Council, which is made up of the CEOs of Canada's top 100 businesses. In 2019, she co-chaired the Business Council Task Force for Canada's Economic Future, leading the way in generating and communicating high-level recommendations to help grow Canada's economy.

As a by-product of all this, Nicole is regularly invited as a keynote speaker to share her story and insights on technology with government agencies and large companies alike. Everything she's done to build her personal brand reinforces the success of her company brand. In her words:

> "I have always been very interested in the bigger picture, in trends, and in thinking about how we grow the entire innovation ecosystem, startups, support women in business, or even how to expand an entire economy. I believe this has helped me operate at a strategic level and helped position me as a thought leader, which in turn has helped position OMX to be a leader in supply chain and social licence across many sectors, particularly the public sector."

LinkedIn: www.linkedin.com/in/nicoleverkindt
Web: https://theomx.com

STEP 2: PUBLISH

When you deliver a compelling pitch, several big questions tend to come up (whether people say them out loud or not). They are thinking:

- Why should I trust you?
- How do I find out more?
- How do I pass on this information?

A lot of people come up with big ideas every day; very few people can attract the right team and get a project to completion. The people you pitch to will want to learn more about the ideas you have and about you too.

People need to know that: you are able to come up with credible insights, and that they can trust your ability to get things done.

Quality published content says a lot about you. A published book, for example, says that you have put enough thought into this idea to have written an entire book on the topic.

Published content online allows people to read your ideas and get to know your story from anywhere in the world. It allows information to be easily passed on without the need for a face-to-face meeting.

Interviews and articles that you've written say that you must either be an expert or have access to experts. We assume that in order to write a quality article you must have some expertise in this field or you must have been able to interview people with expertise.

Very few people create a significant volume of published content. If you have articles, blogs, reports, case studies, and a book, you are much more likely to be perceived as a Key Person of Influence in your industry.

You'd be shocked to know how many of the world's biggest businesses started with published content. Bill Gates wrote articles for his local computer clubs and attracted the first talented employees to Microsoft because of what he wrote.

Sheryl Sandberg (COO, Facebook) wrote the book *Lean In* and is now considered to be the world's most sought-after COO. Richard Branson is dyslexic and manages to release a new book every other year.

COMMIT TO WRITING A BOOK

For the rest of this section I want to encourage you to write a book on your topic. It requires you to produce about 30,000–50,000 words and cover a range of relevant information. You'll write case studies, stories, methods, and all sorts of valuable insights in the process of producing a book.

A published author is often well connected in their field. By writing a book you will be able to pick up the phone and talk to all sorts of new contacts to get input for your book. If you have published something, chances are that you are able to attract the right people around you.

Imagine when you meet people and can say, "I am the author of a book on my industry and while writing the book I discovered a potential business opportunity that I am currently working on."

Now people are interested. This wasn't just anybody who came up with an idea; it was the author of a book. And if this person has what it takes to write a book, they could clearly add value to a business in that field too.

You might be a bit worried about writing an entire book. Maybe you believe you don't have enough content to fill a book; maybe your ideas aren't special enough in your opinion; maybe your ideas aren't worth writing about. These are all concerns that many now-published authors had before sitting down and writing their books and articles.

Our company, Dent Global, has helped nearly 1000 entrepreneurs around the world become published authors. Often these were people who had barely written a blog post before working with us, yet they had a lot of experience in their industries.

If it happens that you fall short of a book, you'll be able to repurpose your content into reports, articles, blogs, handouts, and the like. So for now, set a goal to write a book.

THE ROI ON A PRE-SOLD AUDIENCE

Most business owners spend enormous amounts of time finding, educating, and acquiring customers.

Here's a common scenario:

You're out and about attending client meetings, running errands, and even going to a networking event in the evening.

You happen to meet someone who would potentially make a great client and you set up a meeting (you even get a referral come into your inbox as well—bonus!).

You attend that meeting, get to know the prospect for the first time and they spend time getting to know you. Given they haven't spent much time with you or seen much about you online, a lot of rapport building goes on before you can really talk business.

You leave the meeting, promise to follow up and then engage in a series of phone calls, more meetings and proposals, followed by more follow-up calls.

Sound familiar?

Unfortunately, this is all too common for a lot of business owners (more than will care to admit it). They don't have any scalable and repeatable way to generate, nurture, and warm leads in their sales process.

I was recently sitting down with a group of entrepreneurs talking about the value of producing content. They all recognized that they should be producing more of it, yet they weren't.

The irony of the situation was, they responded by saying they didn't have time because they were too busy finding, prospecting or delivering value to clients. When I pressed them further, the deeper truth was they were overwhelmed by content creation and didn't know where to start.

And I realized, like in my business, that if something isn't directly linked to cash (ROI) it gets bumped down the priority list.

From my perspective, I see content of all forms—written, audio, visual, video—bringing cash into our business (and our clients' businesses) constantly. We couldn't operate at the scale and efficiency we do without it.

Let's look at some examples.

Natasha Hawker runs an employee relations company in Sydney, Australia with fourteen staff. Through the KPI Accelerator, she wrote a book called *From Hire to Fire & Everything in Between*.

It turns out she interviewed a CEO of a top insurance company for her book. When she later published the book, she hand-delivered a copy to him.

She could see he was intrigued, so after a little probing she decided (on the spot) to pitch him on a partnership opportunity. She suggested that the insurer buy a copy of her book for all their small business clients, in exchange for some value-added services she would provide to them.

The CEO loved the idea. That afternoon she'd secured a deal for the insurance company to buy—get this—50,000 copies of her book. Off the back of that book distribution deal, she generated an additional $500,000 in new revenue.

Darren Finkelstein sells power boats in Australia. He wrote the book *Honey, Let's Buy a Boat!* and added an extra $100,000 to his bottom line in the twelve months after he launched his book, simply because more people showed up to his boat yard "pre-sold" on buying a boat.

Rebecca Coomes wrote a book of SIBO recipes and was flown to the USA, all expenses paid, to do a multi-city book tour to share her knowledge.

These are wonderful examples but by no means the exception to the rule. Ultimately, books provide cut-through.

In each of these examples the up-front costs of producing and launching a book are anywhere from one-third to one-tenth of the return our clients typically get within the first twelve months. Try getting an ROI of three to ten times on shares, property—or any other asset, for that matter—within twelve months of purchase. Building and leveraging your own intellectual property is hands-down the most powerful wealth accumulation strategy you can deploy.

This is all before you factor in the indirect deals that get done as an author, the stickiness of your message in the market, and the tools to allow your team to leverage your insights when you're not in the room. The ROI on these is priceless and keeps giving long after you've produced your book.

INNOVATION IS 90% MODELLING, 10% DIFFERENTIATION

With human ingenuity, there's a misconception that we need to totally reinvent ourselves to stand out.

If you think there's already too many KPIs or authors in your field to get cut-through, experience tells me there's not. The reality is, you only need to make a 10% change in direction to be perceived as noticeably different from your competition.

When Virgin Atlantic first launched, they didn't suddenly decide to transport passengers across the Atlantic on hovercrafts instead of planes. They didn't come up with an entirely new flight path, full of acrobatics and rotations for the passengers' amusement. They didn't throw the safety manual out and start from scratch.

The way they differentiated was subtle.

The service was a little friendlier, edgier, and more fun than what people were used to. The food was slightly nicer. The price was a bit cheaper. The boarding process was more pleasant. There were some "surprises and delights" customers weren't expecting. The advertising and branding was a little cheekier, more irreverent. These things dramatically changed the value proposition from everything else that was available at the time.

You sharing your stories, case studies, philosophies, what you stand for and against—these things significantly change how you are perceived in the eyes of your market. Simply packaging those philosophies into beautifully designed reports, blogs, books, and digital tools instantly makes you stand out a cut above the rest in your industry.

With the right frameworks to follow and an environment to keep you accountable, it's a lot simpler than you might think.

DIFFERENT TYPES OF BOOKS

Fortunately, there are a few different types of books you could write and each one has unique benefits.

Here are five types of books you could write:

1. NICHE—THOUGHT LEADERSHIP

This is a book you can write based on your story, your background, and your recommendations for the future.

People who have completed the Key Person of Influence Program have produced books like:

Honey Let's Buy A Boat—Everything you wanted to know about buying (and selling) a recreational power boat but didn't know who to ask

Six Pack Chick—Change your mind, transform your body

Life CEO—Take charge and start doing your life's work, not your busy work

The advantage of this type of book is that it gives you plenty of room to demonstrate your ideas and your unique take on things. You are the star of this kind of book because it's you sharing your specific insights.

2. BOOK OF INTERVIEWS

This is a book where you find existing KPIs and feature their stories or their ideas in a book.

The advantage of this type of book is that it's a great reason for you to get to know existing KPIs in your industry. The disadvantage is that you don't get to be the star of the show. Your KPI status will improve as a person who must be well connected, but not as a thought leader in your own right.

3. BOOK OF TIPS

This is a book full of quick tips and rapid-fire ideas. A great example is one of our clients, JP Devilliers, who wrote *77 Ways To Reshape Your Life*.

He's a fitness trainer who had limited time between clients in the gym. He allocated three short slots throughout his busy day to note down a tip and by the end of the month he had his book.

List the ten main categories of interest you want to cover then come up with ten tips for each category. Now you will have 100 tips; if you write three tips per day it will take you less than two months to complete the book.

4. PICTURE BOOK

For some industries, showing lots of pictures might be more effective. Clearly if you are a photographer or a fashion designer, people would be much more interested in your pictures than words.

One of the KPI Program clients, John Cassidy, is one of the

world's top headshot photographers. His book *Headshots: Your personal brand and the 7 mistakes to avoid* is a series of before and after photos that illustrate the difference between a great headshot and a poor one.

He's put in his tips and his philosophies, and this short picture book serves as a perfect business tool.

5. A CREATIVE PIECE

This could be a parable with a message or a fictional story. The advantages are that you get full licence to make up as much as you like and that it's very much an expression of your creativity. People love creative books; fiction massively outsells non-fiction.

A good example is the book *If Your Body Could Talk: Letters from your body to you* by Jacquie Sharples. It takes the form of a series of letters written from a woman's body to the woman who "owns" it. The book is powerful and compelling. It works because Jacquie is a gifted writer and her message isn't lost in this format—if anything it's amplified.

The downside is that few people are skilled enough as writers to get this genre right, and it has little value to you as a Key Person of Influence if the message doesn't come across.

THE MESSAGE OF THE BOOK

Once you have decided on the type of book you will produce, it is very important to consider the message you want your reader to walk away with. My writing coach says that a great book must answer at least one significant question that the reader is trying to answer.

Your readers may be asking themselves:

"How do I have difficult conversations with an employee?"

"How do people become wealthy, starting from scratch?"

"How do I protect my valuable business ideas?"

The reader's core question forms the theme of your book, and each chapter, interview, or section is giving another key piece of information that answers this question.

PLANNING THE BOOK

Before you even lay your fingers on the keyboard to start writing your book, you must plan your book.

When you plan your book, you put the key question on a large piece of paper and brainstorm all of the connected questions people in your micro-niche might ask. Explore the content you need to share with them to fully answer their questions.

The planning and writing process makes you smarter on your topic. It forces you to formulate vague thoughts into clear, articulate, and tangible ideas that will spread.

CHOOSING THE TITLE OF YOUR BOOK

Whatever type of book you produce, one of the most important decisions is the title. Many more people will hear that you are the author of *The Title You Chose* than those who actually read the book.

You might like to call your book something vague that only makes perfect sense once read to the end. However, your book will lose impact with a cryptic title. If you introduce yourself as, "I am the author of the book *The Race*," people can't tell the field in which you are a Key Person of Influence. If you introduce yourself as "the author of *The Race Towards Green Energy*," people instantly understand that you must be a KPI for green issues.

My belief is that you should choose a title that reinforces that you are a Key Person of Influence. It should be brand-enhancing and you should feel proud to tell people that you are the author of that book.

Some of the great book titles created on the KPI Accelerator by our clients are:

Legally Branded—Shireen Smith

Winning Client Trust—Chris Davies

Profit From Payroll—Tracy Angwin

The Smart Business Exit—Geoff Green

Me Time—Kate Christie

OMG! I'm Getting a Divorce—Caralee Caldwell

The Suit Book—Clare Sheng

All of these titles have been perfect for getting across the message that the author is a Key Person of Influence in their chosen field.

ENVIRONMENT DICTATES PERFORMANCE

Some people love the idea of going away to a writing retreat in the quiet foothills of a picturesque location. Before you do that, I recommend first getting a writing coach or joining a writing group so you have access to feedback, accountability, and guidance.

The perfect writing environment is more about accountability and feedback than the scenery.

The Key Person of Influence Accelerator program runs all over the world and has a high success rate for getting people to perfect their pitch and then turn it into a book in a matter of a few months.

People who join the Key Person of Influence Accelerator are provided with coaching, mentoring, and accountability through the book-writing process, and many are shocked to find they have a completed first draft in under thirty days.

As with anything challenging, being part of the right environment is half the battle. You want to be part of an environment that normalizes the result you are seeking.

If you want to be better at tennis, join a tennis club or get a tennis coach. If you want to make more money, hang out with people who earn lots of money. If you want to write a book, get around people who are also writing a book.

The accountability of having someone coaching you and being part of a group who are all writing is a powerful formula for getting your book out.

There is a lot to learn about writing a book and getting it selling. It's worth working with someone who's done it before. So many people say they are "working on a book" but few actually get it published.

Don't get caught in the trap of getting halfway through several book ideas; a book has no power until it's finished. A writing program can help you to get your book completed and on Amazon in under six months rather than thirty-six months (or never). Imagine what an extra thirty months of being a Key Person of Influence is worth.

If you would like to fast-track your way to becoming a Key Person of Influence in your industry, then head here: www.kpidiagnostic.com

PUBLISHING YOUR BOOK

In the past, getting a publishing deal was an essential part of becoming an author. Only publishing houses had the money and the power to print a large quantity of books and then get them distributed. Today there are printers and publishers who will print your book in very small runs on demand. There's no reason you can't print just twenty copies of your book at a time.

Rethink Press—the publisher of this book—is an example of one of those boutique publishers. They're known as a "hybrid" publisher, which means they provide a lot of the flexibility and benefits of self-publishing without the restrictive conditions a traditional publisher places on most new authors.

You can Google "hybrid publishers" or "Rethink Press" to learn more. There are many fast and low-cost options that enable people to publish their own books nowadays.

PROMOTING YOUR BOOK

There are many ways to promote your book if you want to focus on marketing. However, it is not vital that your book is a massive seller; it is more important that you are an author.

Each year less than a dozen books sell over a million copies. Most books don't sell more than 500 copies a year.

That's fine; if you use your book correctly it won't need to sell millions. The mere fact that you are an author and that people can see you on Amazon gives you more kudos and opportunities.

You will find that it is easier to get invited to speak, to get publicity in the media, and to get face-to-face with key contacts once you are an author. Being an author helps you to become much more recognized and credible.

When you meet people you can gift them a copy of your book (a book is the best business card there is). You can give your existing clients several copies to give to their friends. Strategically giving books can make you more money than selling them.

Remember, it is not authors who get great opportunities, it is KPIs. Your goal is to become the Key Person of Influence in your industry in under twelve months, not to spend all your energy trying to sell books. Without all five steps in the KPI Method, you'll miss out on the bigger picture.

The purpose of your book is to promote you, not the other way around.

BEING AN AUTHOR ALONE DOESN'T MAKE YOU A KEY PERSON OF INFLUENCE

Unfortunately, I meet a lot of authors who have a book but they're not making much money.

They might point to the KPI Method or what I wrote earlier in this chapter and say, "But I did what you said and became an author." While being an author gives you authority over a subject matter, it doesn't guarantee success on its own.

A reputation as a Key Person of Influence comes from your ability to deliver the outcome your book promises. You must be able to consistently deliver a transformation to your clients. Ideas are worthless if they're not backed up by remarkable implementation.

This comes in the form of an ecosystem of products and services that can take your target market from where they are now to where they want to be.

Ultimately, you must fundamentally change your customer's life (or organization) by transforming their current situation. In the Key Person of Influence Accelerator, we call this delivering a full and remarkable solution to your customers' problems.

A book allows you to start a conversation, but becoming a Key Person of Influence means you must also bring home remarkable transformations for your clients as well.

YOU'RE STILL 1 IN 1000

Seeing a handful or even dozens of visible authors and Key People of Influence in your industry can really psych an entrepreneur out before they've even started.

For every author, influencer or KPI you spot on Instagram or Facebook, there are 1000 other worker-bees (more on this later) competing against one another. When you take into account your market size, there could be dozens of industry authors in your country—or even city—alone, and there would still be plenty of room for everyone to enjoy a nice slice of the pie.

Key People of Influence don't have a fixed mindset when it comes to mobilizing resources in their industry. In fact, through strategic partnerships and joint ventures (which we'll cover in the next few chapters), they see other KPIs as their greatest allies.

Remember, 10% of every industry is made up of Key People of Influence. You simply need to be one of them.

After working with 3000 founders around the world, we've discovered the list of potential micro-niches is nearly endless. With focus, resilience, and hard work, it's entirely possible to apply the KPI Method to almost any micro-niche and build a profitable lifestyle business as a result.

PUBLISHING ARTICLES

As I mentioned, the reason I've focused on writing a book up until now is because once you have the content written you can repurpose it in many ways.

You can chop up your 30,000-word book into a series of articles, handouts, and blogs once you're done. Of course you could also approach things the other way around and write articles and blogs first, and later use these as chapters in your book. An article, if published in the right place, can be incredibly powerful for building your brand and communicating with your market.

One of the KPI Accelerator clients, Paul Fowler, owns a flight school and published a set of articles about his WWII Spitfire Project. He had a goal to build a squadron of replica Spitfires and the articles were instrumental in finding other interested parties and making it a reality.

Writing these articles forced him to get very clear about his ideas and gave him an excuse to interview relevant KPIs in his industry. After his articles were published in a boutique flying magazine, he was able to send copies to his existing clients and gain the credibility that comes with being published in an industry magazine.

Be sure to collect any publications you are in, scan the front page along with your contribution, and put it on your website and on your social media profiles.

PUBLISHING CREATES CREDIBILITY—PRODUCTS CREATE CASH

Your books, articles, blogs or reports will be brilliant tools for getting your thinking clear, for getting recognized as credible, and for connecting to the right people. However, there's not much money in it directly.

Well-designed products are the key to making money, so rather than pushing yourself to sell more books or to get paid as a writer, let's move along and explore how to create hot products that bring in the money.

Are you ready for the next step?

In the next chapter you will see that a great product can be high-value, low-cost, and open up all sorts of opportunities.

If you are ready to turn your skill set into an asset, read on.

ACTION STEP

For some additional content on this step visit:
https://ca.dent.global/publish/

CASE STUDY: MICHEL FALCON,
CO-FOUNDER OF BARO AND PETTY CASH

Michel Falcon runs his 150-person businesses in one of the most competitive industries in the world—the hospitality industry. His two restaurants, Baro and Petty Cash, are some of the most iconic food and beverage institutions in Toronto.

However, Michel isn't just known for being a restaurateur. Far from it. His origin story as an entrepreneur truly dates back to his time as a sales rep with junk removal business 1-800-GOT-JUNK. Now a $250M+ consortium of brands, 1-800-GOT-JUNK (founded by Vancouver-based entrepreneur, Brian Scudamore) ingrained a philosophy of taking care of employees first, in order to take care of company profits —not the other way around.

This reinforced what he came to believe from a young age:

> "In my early 20s, as my career was just getting started, I came across a *Harvard Business Review* article that described a strategy that I had never heard of before. That strategy was customer experience management. This was my eureka moment, when I made the connection that every admired brand had a customer experience strategy. Soon after, I realized that you can't have strong customer experience efforts if you don't have an employee engagement plan."

Thanks to his experience at 1-800-GOT-JUNK, Michel became obsessed with employee engagement. He approached and interviewed the CEOs of some of the world's most celebrated companies in order to study the habits and best practices that made their people (and companies) thrive. In the course of these interviews, Michel developed and formalized his own intellectual property around why putting people at the heart of an organization's strategy is one of the most predictable pathways to success.

When I asked Michel, "What do you do?" his answer was simple and clear:

> "I make people feel safe by building 'People First Cultures' into the fabric of every organization I'm a part of. My restaurants Baro and Petty Cash serve a team of over 150 people, who in turn serve thousands of our patrons in order to produce profitable businesses in an industry where profits are rare."

Throughout that whole period, Michel had been publishing his findings on channels like LinkedIn and his own blog. Large companies were taking notice, and before long he was being invited all over the world to speak and share his message with powerful audiences. Some of the world's biggest brands hired Michel to consult with their companies on how they, too, could build a thriving company by building a thriving culture.

In 2018 this led Michel to publish his first book, *People First Culture—Build a lasting company by shifting your focus from profits to people.* Taking over ten years of obsessive study and experimentation through his own companies, Michel has codified the blueprint for how any company in any industry can win by implementing a People First Culture.

Since the release of the book, demand for Michel's keynote speaking and consulting services have skyrocketed. Thanks to the book and every interaction leading to it, Michel has established a clear position for himself in the market as a Key Person of Influence in employee engagement and company culture. Today, people are sharing and implementing the People First Culture methodology within their own organizations and profiting as a result. Most importantly, they're making more money while also improving the lives of their people. Michel said:

> "Publishing a book has boosted my profile enormously. It's allowed my message to spread and opened doors I simply wouldn't have expected before writing it."

LinkedIn: www.linkedin.com/in/michelfalcon
Web: www.michelfalcon.com
Amazon: Search "People First Culture: Build a lasting company by shifting your focus from profits to people"

HALFWAY POINT

How are you going with the hidden theme I mentioned in the Introduction?

The theme I'm talking about is something you are very close to; maybe it's something you've taken for granted until now.

Consider this theme I'm talking about has everything to do with your story and this book may only be a tool for finding it.

Maybe the theme I'm referring to started long before you even picked up this book. Look back in the early chapters, see what you can remember.

Keep looking, do the exercises and if needed, re-read this book a few times until you get it.

For now, let's continue your journey as a Key Person of Influence. The next step, "Product," is a powerful and important part of the process.

STEP 3: PRODUCT

Money moves toward hot products.

Why does Apple have lots of money? For over ten years they have produced very hot products. If they fail to do that in the future the money will dry up for them.

Why do oil and gas companies have lots of money? For over 100 years oil and gas have been very hot products. If we create more solar energy technology, the oil and gas companies will lose their hot products and they will lose their money.

What about you? The reason you've made money in the past is because of products too. Maybe you started by selling your time to an employer. Maybe you then started selling services to your clients. Maybe you've made money buying and selling a house. Any of these money-makers were actually about products. Your time was a product that an employer wanted, your services produced something your clients wanted, and your house went up in value as it was seen to be an increasingly hotter product.

Maybe in the future you'll have other products to sell that you've not yet created. Maybe your business will sell products that are so hot you'll make more money than you can spend in your lifetime. Maybe you'll sell your business systems as a product in the form of a franchise or a licence.

Your business will really take off when you have several products that spread your message and expand your income opportunities.

PRODUCT ECOSYSTEMS

Here's a powerful idea to consider:

Products and services don't make money;
products and service ecosystems do.
#kpimethod

Your business will really take off when you have a mix of products and services that all work together to maximize the value exchange in every customer relationship.

Businesses that make lots of money can't always put their finger on which product makes them the money. They give away some digital products for free, some things they sell cheaply, some products or services are high value but they only sell to warm prospects who had the free product.

Imagine if Google started charging for searches, maps, or browsers. They'd probably lose their market share. It makes sense for them to give some things away and charge for others.

Some products are designed to build a relationship. Some products are designed to educate. Some products are designed to implement an idea.

All products are based upon your insights.

PRODUCTS ARE PACKAGED-UP IDEAS

Two hundred years ago the wealthiest people owned tracts of land and sprawling farms. One hundred years ago the wealthiest people owned massive factories and bustling production lines. Today the wealthiest people have big ideas that spread like wildfire.

We now live in a global economy that is largely intangible and centres on ideas. The successful people who make money and win the accolades are the people who have powerful ideas and can turn them into products.

The most valuable commodity on the planet today is called "Intellectual Property" (IP). The biggest companies on the planet are valued almost entirely on their IP.

A product is merely a valuable insight or an idea that has been packaged up so that people can access it easily, repeatedly, and in a desirable way.

We live in a time when products are the new marketing and advertising tools. In the past, companies would make fairly generic products and then spend a fortune telling the world that they were the best.

Today that doesn't work. People have learned to tune out loud advertising and go looking for great products instead.

One of my favourite authors, Seth Godin, says that:

"Finding new ways, more clever ways, to interrupt people doesn't work. It's the person who knows how to create an idea that spreads that wins today."

Rather than over-spending on ads, the better way is to create better products that people want to access and tell their friends about.

If you create a valuable product, your customers and clients will tweet, share, blog, update, and like it publicly, and do your marketing for you.

DIGITAL PRODUCTS

One of the best ways you can really share your ideas with a vast number of people in an effective way is to create a digital product; this will likely be a download or an online tool. Such products are not an interruption, they are a means of communication that consumers chose to participate in.

If packaged correctly, these products have a high perceived value, even though the cost to reproduce them is almost nothing.

If someone takes an hour to listen to your audio podcast, they build rapport with you, they bond with you, and they start to understand what makes you unique.

If someone spends two hours watching your well-produced videos on Facebook or YouTube, they've already begun to buy into your ideas. If someone joins your online community, attends your Facebook Live session, or takes your online test, they are spending time and getting to know you.

You start becoming the person they *must* do business with rather than a person they *could* do business with. You shift from functional to vital.

PRODUCTIZED SERVICES

A service can be packaged up like a product. You can give your service a name, it can have a method, it can have a brochure, it can be delivered by other trained professionals. This productized service could include elements that are standardized and elements that are bespoke.

Don't fall into the trap of thinking you deliver a service and this step can't apply to you. Treat your service like a product and you'll see an uplift.

A plastic surgeon who joined the KPI Accelerator thought he would struggle with product creation because it doesn't get more bespoke than performing surgery. He was (legally) able to give his method a name, create brochures, compile stories, and add additional products into the overall bundle. As a result, his value went up and his waiting list grew.

Your service is part of the product ecosystem, so be sure to make it as productized as you can and to surround it with other products that help educate, inspire, or relate to more people.

PRODUCTS EXPAND YOUR INCOME OPPORTUNITIES

Imagine that you get invited to be a guest speaker for thirty minutes at an industry conference.

You agree, on the condition that you can promote your digital product for $50. At the end of the talk, you say, "If you like what you just heard and you want to know a little more, I have a special offer for my online training program."

If twenty people out of the group decide to buy, you just got paid $1000 for a thirty-minute speaking spot: a great result.

This is also likely to lead to a lot more business. Each person who buys the first product is more likely to want to do business with you in the future as well.

PRODUCTS FREE YOU FROM THE TIME-FOR-MONEY TRAP

If *you* are your only product, being paid for your time, this presents a big problem. There will always be a limitation on what you can earn if your earning capacity is based solely on your personal attendance.

Selling your time may still be part of what you do, but when you have an ecosystem of digital products and productized services the value of your time goes up, not down. A chef who sells a lot of recipe books makes more money for their time even though everyone has access to the recipes.

Don't think, however, that creating products means you don't have to show up...

ONLY KEY PEOPLE OF INFLUENCE EXPERIENCE "PASSIVE INCOME"

One of the common things we hear entrepreneurs say is they want a business that gives them passive income. The harsh reality is: thinking about income as "passive" is liable to set most business owners up for an emotional struggle that's simply not worth it.

There's a little part of the human brain that wants to be able to sit back, relax, and watch cash roll into our bank accounts with little input or effort from us. It's the monkey mind wishing business and life could just be easy, but ultimately this is a fantasy that doesn't serve the vast majority of entrepreneurs.

Let me explain why.

Yes, it's true that income often comes into my bank account when I didn't touch the sale and have no idea who the customer is. Richard Branson certainly isn't ringing the cash register on your Virgin Atlantic ticket or greeting you as you board a Virgin train. Jeff Bezos is so far removed from the money that flows into Amazon's bank account that some employees might even wonder if he still works for Amazon.

In all of these examples, none of these entrepreneurs are energetically leaning "out" of their business. On the contrary, as Key People of Influence they're the life-force behind their organizations.

If Richard Branson weren't actively championing the mission, vision, and values of Virgin, the empire would very quickly come crumbling down. If Jeff Bezos weren't constantly expanding into new markets and exploring new frontiers, Amazon's growth would come to a grinding halt.

It is because of these entrepreneurs and their inspired visions for the future that people are attracted to work with their companies. It is because of their energy and unique insights that customers keep coming back to do business with them.

The reason Dent is able to operate in four cities around the world, with a team of over forty people across eight time zones, is because the founders are "leaning in." If any one of us were to sit back on a beach for an extended period of time while everyone else was working, the life-force would drain from our organization very rapidly.

Great people want to align with resourceful, inspiring leaders—not anonymous profit takers.

SO WHAT *IS* PASSIVE INCOME AS AN ENTREPRENEUR?

Income flows from assets.

When you develop a powerful message, write books, and create hot products, all of a sudden there will be situations where you experience what feels like passive income.

You will be invited as a paid speaker to talk to a group of your perfect target market to whom you would have happily presented for free.

You will have other leaders show up and want to help build your business in their local market when you're on the other side of the world.

You will have team-creating business assets like manuals, brochures, websites, and systems that build the valuation of your business without you being involved.

Passive income exists—but only for the entrepreneurs that are leaning into being the Key People of Influence that continuously breathe energy and vitality into every corner of their organizations.

EVERY BUSINESS HAS IDEAS BEHIND IT

You may be wondering how "product thinking" applies to a more traditional business like accounting, printing, consulting, or logistics. Should these more unglamorous businesses create digital and information products for their clients too? Absolutely *yes*.

Regardless of the business, it is the ideas behind your business that make it special and prevent you from having to constantly compete on price.

In order for any business to stand out from the crowd, it needs to have some great underpinning ideas. People want to know what sets you apart or, at the very least, what is "your take on things," before they get excited about you and feel happy to spend a little more.

Imagine a dry cleaner who gave you an app that told you what to do immediately if you stained your clothes. You'd keep that app on your phone and you'd think about your dry cleaner as soon as you spilled something on your shirt.

Imagine a men's fashion outlet that had an online video series featuring an image consultant sharing ideas on *How To Look Slimmer, Richer and More Powerful For Less Than $500*. Instantly you start thinking about spending $500 in that store.

Imagine a restaurant that had a report from the chef based on her commitment to sustainable, ethical farming. You'd talk to your foodie friends about it.

Just seeing a report called *Why I choose to pay more for my ingredients so that you can feel good about your meal* would make you feel good about paying a little more at the end of your night.

No matter what industry you are in, you need to share the ideas that make you unique. Explain to people what's so special about the way you deliver your service. Give them a peek behind the curtain at some of the things you take for granted but your customers never knew.

The clients I've worked with have produced things they never knew they could, and it transformed their businesses. They've created events, trainings, books, online tests, podcasts, apps, and many other products that are designed to spread the word while making money.

WHAT IF YOU SELL A COMMODITY?

If you sell a widget or some other commoditized product and don't think you can differentiate it, stop and consider these questions:

- What beliefs do you have about life or your industry?
- What did you want to be when you grew up?
- What irks you about the world? What frustrates you?
- What makes you come alive?
- What maxims or principles do you live by?

Hidden within these seemingly off-topic questions are some of the ingredients that will make you and your business stand out. When you can "connect the dots" of who you are, you can build a vision, message, and ecosystem of products that are an expression of you.

This business contains your unique DNA. It can't be replicated.

Sam Buckby ran an electrical business in Australia just like every other electrical business and couldn't figure out how to differentiate. He'd been grinding away at it for twelve years.

It turned out he had a passion for new tech and "smart homes." He firmly believed home automation was the future of the construction industry.

We helped Sam develop his IP in this area, and as a result he wrote a book called *Homes with a Heartbeat*. This led to him creating a whole new home automation advisory product with 600% higher profit margins than the same electrical business in its best year.

There is a unique essence waiting to be unlocked and woven through your pitch, your messaging, your products, your online profile, and your partnerships.

Don't underestimate the mountain you're already standing on.

TWO TYPES OF PRODUCTS

There are several types of products that can be useful for your business.

The real uplift in income comes from several products and services that all work together. A "product ecosystem" creates a lot more money than any one product or service on its own.

There are two types of products you'll need to develop:

- Products built for high volume to develop relationships.
- Products built to deliver high value and drive profit.

Let's take a look at these two types of products.

START WITH PRODUCTS THAT SPREAD IDEAS

Everyone should have a free product. The person who will dominate your industry in the next ten years will be the one who is able to give more away for free than anyone else. The fastest-growing companies in the 2000s were all companies that gave away incredible value for free—Google, Facebook, Twitter, LinkedIn.

The best thing you can give away for free is an information product that educates people as to why they should do business with you. Here are some examples:

A FREE PODCAST

A podcast is a remarkable way to engage with your target market, and as a medium it is experiencing explosive growth globally. When people listen to your podcast they are thinking, "This person really knows their stuff" or "This person is super connected" and they naturally begin to know, like, and trust you, and want to do business with you. They can also do this in 'NET' time (No Extra Time). Meaning that they could be driving the car, cleaning the house, or going to the gym all while building a relationship with you and your brand.

There's nothing you can create more cheaply that has more value than an information product that shares your experience and insights with your potential clients. A podcast is free, it's valuable, it's global, and it's fast. There's already a global audience downloading podcasts just waiting for yours to arrive.

A VIDEO CHANNEL

Today, in our pockets we all carry a high-quality video camera that you would have needed a suitcase to transport only a decade ago.

Through platforms like Upwork and Freelancer, it's easy to find people anywhere in the world to edit your raw footage, adding overlays, graphics, and images to give your amateur video a professional look and feel.

These videos can then be uploaded to platforms with a global audience of people just waiting to consume what you have to say. Facebook Watch, YouTube, Instagram, and IGTV are the new television stations and they're only just getting started.

AN ONLINE SCORECARD TOOL

Today we live in a world where it's possible to generate data-rich leads cheaply and easily. What marketers only dreamed of ten years ago is now available at the click of a button.

Online quizzes and scorecards are valuable products for your market to use, giving people deep and personalized insights into their problems and current situations. Often these tools produce beautiful reports, giving your prospects immense value for free.

Companies like www.scoreapp.com have invested big money into building software-as-a-service (SaaS) platforms enabling business owners like you to automatically generate their own quiz and scorecard tools for as little as a couple of hundred dollars a month.

HERE'S A SECRET... SHARE YOUR SECRETS!

Here's a big secret: Don't keep secrets. Share your best ideas with everyone.

Consider that the most famous chefs share their recipes every week. The more they share, the more their value goes through the roof. You don't hear people saying, "Now I have Gordon Ramsay's recipe, I will never visit any of his restaurants again."

The more people have, the more they want, so share your ideas freely. You will also make room in your mind to have even better ideas.

If you share powerful ideas, people will come to you to implement them and you can have a valuable service offering that does that.

NICHE PRODUCTS ARE HIGHER VALUE

People spend a lot of time and money producing weak or average products that just lack value because they are too general.

If you create a product that helps solve a very real and specific challenge that people have, it will perform.

If you want to sell an information kit on some general subject like *How to be a good parent*, it probably won't stand out.

If, however, you hone your micro-niche and create a product like *How to be an amazing single parent while still working your high-pressure, city job*, you will find that parents facing this challenge will beat down your door.

A product that solves a specific problem is seen as valuable; if it's too general it seldom gets traction.

HIGH-VALUE PRODUCTS

After you've experimented with high-volume products that get you known and spread ideas, you'll naturally want to create high-value products that generate serious profit.

IMPLEMENTATION, NOT IDEAS

Information is so readily available that its value has fallen considerably. Up until the 2000s, people would buy information and place a high price on it. They would pay for CD sets, seminars, videos, documents, reports, and the like. Today all of those are freely available on any smart phone, so they're not something people will pay a lot for—if anything.

The real money comes from offering an implementation solution. At the same time as information has fallen in value, the value of getting something done for you has risen. People are time poor and drowning in options.

They want trusted suppliers who can get things done for them. This is where your "productized service" comes in to implement the ideas you've given away freely in your other products.

As I mentioned, a top chef can give away recipes and, strangely, it drives demand for their restaurant. People read the recipe and then want the food made for them.

It's the same in most industries. One of our KPI Accelerator clients is a respected intellectual property lawyer. We helped her create several information products and write a book. As a result, hundreds of people want her firm to advise on their businesses and she's created a productized service to streamline that process and to make her service available to people all over the world.

Another KPI Accelerator client is a chiropractor. He used to sell his time by the hour and each session he would work hard to rebook the client. Working with us, he created a product package that included his services and the services of several other wellness professionals. This product gets better results for clients and all four practitioners are now selling the services of each other every time they sign on a client to this product.

The key to these high-value products is that they are focused on implementation rather than ideas.

We personally give away a lot of ideas in our books, blogs, articles, webinars, and events. We know that when the time comes for people to implement these ideas they will want to work with us.

INTUITION IS SIMPLY UNEXAMINED PROCESS

I hear a lot of entrepreneurs say to me, "I'm stuck doing client work because my clients only want to work with me." Or they can't find anyone with their level of experience or expertise to replace them. If they did find someone brilliant, it would take years to train them up to their level.

Sound familiar?

But what they don't realize is their clients don't care about them. Their clients only care about what's in their heads.

When you do the work you're good at, your brain sends and receives signals quickly. Really quickly.

But it didn't start out that way. You first had to develop conscious competence in your new area of expertise. Deliberate practice. Then, after thousands of hours of honing your craft, you became highly competent and efficient at delivering powerful results to your clients.

Much like an algorithm, your brain and body just go to work on autopilot. You know the right questions to ask, in what order, and the right things to say and do to solve your clients' problems with remarkable efficacy. It all happens intuitively.

How do you replicate that?

Well, beneath that intuition is simply a series of steps. Steps that have become so smooth and so refined over time that they appear to happen by some difficult-to-define intuition.

When we slow our clients down and force them to unpack their IP through a series of frameworks, they see that there's a far more systemic and repeatable approach to what they do. It then becomes possible to "map" the system and start to transfer the components from you to other people with specialized expertise, systems, and technology.

Like a automated production line, the result often gets delivered with even more potency—but all of a sudden it relies far less on the founder's input.

When you can free yourself from the bondage of your intuition, you finally have the ability to focus on "productizing" your skills.

Don't fool yourself into thinking you can become a Key Person of Influence without this—otherwise you will be perpetually stuck playing small.

MAKE A PRODUCT FOR YOUR COMPETITORS

There's also a lot of intellectual property that you take for granted that your "competitors" or counterparts (people like you who operate in different markets) would be interested in.

Maybe your restaurant business is great at saving money on wasted food because you have a clever system you came up with. That product could earn you more profit than your restaurant does!

Maybe your business has a smart strategy for generating more warm referrals than the industry norm. That referral generation product could be a game-changer for you.

The Key Person of Influence Scorecard tool is a hot product we developed to help entrepreneurs score themselves in each of the five areas of the KPI Method.

You can take the scorecard here: www.scalemyinfluence.com

It was such a hot product we decided to buy the IT company that developed it for us, and now we sell this as a product to our competitors for a very nice profit.

There are so many ways you can create valuable products in your business with the right product creation methodology to guide you.

MULTIPLY YOUR BUSINESS VALUATION

A business is valued using a formula: *Value = Profit x Multiple.*

For a business that owns its own unique products, that multiple is much higher than for a business that simply sells a service or brokers other people's products.

If ever you have a desire to sell your business or raise investment, you'll get a better valuation thanks to the work you've done in creating hot products.

TO DO THE WORK YOU LOVE, YOU HAVE TO WIN THE WORK

One final point when it comes to creating products:

Everyone gets into business because they think they can do a damn good job at looking after clients. Most people start a business because they worked for an "idiot" who just didn't understand how to deliver value. Very few people start a business because they think they can become better at winning the work. Many businesses are started based on delivery capability; few businesses are started based on sales skills.

Here's the problem: In order to do the work, you need to win the work. You have to get a client to transfer the money, sign the cheque, or enter their PIN. Until that happens, it doesn't matter how good you are at delivering value to your clients.

There's no easy sales system that generates clients passively. Great companies with billion-dollar brands still need excellent sales professionals to secure new business.

Starting a podcast, writing a book, and developing valuable online tools all lubricate the sales process. But they don't eliminate the need for you to sit down with potential clients and take them through a sales conversation.

Your business will always have to win business, you'll always have times when it's hard to meet targets (if you have the ambition to grow) and it never ends.

As soon as you accept this idea, winning business becomes fun. You can come up with great ways to surprise and delight people, and you can create brilliant presentations and work on your communication skills. You can inspire a team of people who help win business and you can find your own groove when selling.

In the next chapter we make you "web-famous" so that when someone googles you, they can see straight away you are a Key Person of Influence and they can begin to get excited to connect.

If you are ready to open up to opportunities all over the planet, turn to the next chapter and read on (after you complete the exercises, of course).

ACTION STEPS

For bonus content relating to this step visit:
https://ca.dent.global/product/

EXERCISES

- What will your first podcast (or next one) be about?
- If you had a training workshop that people would pay $500 for, what would it teach people?
- What are the valuable insights that you could share on a downloadable report?
- What product could you sell to your competitors?

NOTES ...

CASE STUDY: JAYSON GAIGNARD, FOUNDER OF MASTERMIND TALKS

When I met Jayson Gaignard for the first time, it was clear he was in his "element." Naturally charismatic, it was easy to connect the dots behind why he is now known as a super-connector of the world's most fascinating and influential entrepreneurs.

His business Mastermind Talks (MMT) runs a once-a-year, invite-only three-day event, generating seven figures in revenue and featuring a 150-strong list of past and present guests like Gary Vaynerchuk of VaynerMedia; Tim Ferriss, author of *The 4-hour Work Week;* Ryan Holiday, author of *The Obstacle is the Way* and *Ego is the Enemy;* James Altucher, entrepreneur, investor, and author of *Choose Yourself;* and Dave Asprey of the "Bulletproof Diet"... just to name a few.

To say Jayson Gaignard is a Key Person of Influence in highly curated, bespoke events for entrepreneurs is, well, an understatement...

However, it wasn't always this way. Prior to starting Mastermind Talks, Jayson described himself as "Bankrupt on every level. Emotionally, spiritually, financially, and even physically."

> "Just a few years ago, I was stuck on the entrepreneurial 'hamster wheel' building a business I hated, to buy things I didn't need, to impress people I didn't even like. I was successful on the outside, but the heaviness of that success left me yearning for the lightness of being a beginner again."

He decided to close the doors on his previous business, Tickets Canada, which at the height of its growth had a team of twenty people, and start over. Within just a few years he had run his first MMT event with some of the world's most influential entrepreneurs.

How did he do it?

At every interaction, Jayson has an unparalleled ability to connect and form deep and lasting relationships. His philosophy of "give" first, spot opportunity for others, and being a catalyst for collaboration goes to the heart of what forming partnerships in business is all about.

When you look to create opportunity for others first by sharing your resources, the by-product is opportunity in kind. However, it's one thing to be liked by people, it's another to be able to have them pay $10,000+ to attend a three-day event. What allowed him to do that? He puts it down to how he was able to form relationships with the "speakers" and guests in attendance.

> "When I decided to close the doors on Tickets Canada and pursue a new direction, I was hoping to wind down the business gradually and create a soft landing with cash in the bank for the next venture. Through circumstances outside my control, I ended up closing the doors with $250,000 in debt. By this point, I was at 'rock bottom.' Then one very early morning I saw Tim Ferriss post a launch campaign to sell his latest book *The 4-Hour Chef*. He had one package to buy 4000 books in exchange for two speaking engagements. In that moment, I came up with the idea of running a highly curated entrepreneur event with

Tim as the headline speaker. I called three friends, pitched the idea, and raised the $85,000 USD I needed to buy the books. From there, our first MMT event was born."

This helped MMT become one of the hottest products out there in the entrepreneur space. With such an influential guestlist, a rejection rate higher than Harvard University, and an unparalleled "community-driven experience," MMT is a product so good people are beating down the door in droves to gain access to the 150 seats available (more than 15,000 since he started, to be precise).

Today, Jayson is one of the most well-known and well-liked entrepreneurs in Canada. Within a few short years he established himself as a Key Person of Influence by harnessing the power of connection, relationships, great product design, and partnership.

In this time he also authored *Mastermind Dinners: Build lifelong relationships by connecting experts, influencers, and linchpins* which has had more than 190 5-star reviews on Amazon.

All these things have created an echochamber of credibility, authority, and influence for Jayson within a highly exclusive community.

LinkedIn: www.linkedin.com/in/jaysongaignard
Mastermind Talks: http://mmt.community/
Community-made Podcast: http://communitymade.com/
Amazon: Search "Mastermind Dinners: Build lifelong relationships by connecting experts, influencers, and linchpins"

CASE STUDY: ALAN SMITH, FOUNDER OF STRATEGYZER

I first met Alan Smith at an invite-only dinner hosted by Jayson Gaignard of Mastermind Talks in Toronto. When Alan mentioned his company and what they did, I instantly knew a lot about him through the success of his books.

Alan co-founded a company called Strategyzer, which is a leading online course, platform, and training provider for SMEs and large enterprises. Strategyzer is best known for producing business model and value proposition design tools, like the Business Model Canvas and Value Proposition Canvas. These tools have helped more than five million companies around the world both test and develop robust business model and value proposition strategies.

As I learned more about how Alan and his co-founder built their company, I could see they were, among many other things, leveraging the principles outlined in this book.

Their first book *Business Model Generation* was co-created by 470 practitioners from around the world to both research and refine the Business Model Canvas. This tool has taken on a life of its own, being used in millions of organizations and universities all over the globe.

The mistake a lot of small business owners make is believing they need to be the sole creator of value when formalizing their intellectual property or designing products. Alan and his team recognized the value in partnering with other highly credible professionals to co-create and refine the tools outlined in their book. As a result, those people (and the institutions they represent) also become the "evangelists" of the methodologies and help spread the word farther and wider.

Key People of Influence recognize that to reach more people and have greater impact with their message, they must turn their ideas into valuable products as well. After going for a long walk with Alan in downtown Toronto to learn more about his story, I got to hear first-hand how they scaled out their IP.

"After the success of publishing the book we decided to turn the Business Model Canvas into an app so people could use the tool on tablets, which were just starting to take off at the time. We partnered with a developer who shared our vision and took on the risk for the project by forgoing up-front fees. We agreed to pay them only once the product had sold enough to recoup their investment. Thankfully, the app gained hundreds of thousands of downloads around the world in the coming years. The developer got repaid quickly and we generated a healthy profit too."

When I asked Alan how Strategyzer came to evolve into the thriving organization it is today, he said:

"We had a small button in the right hand corner of the app asking customers "what they wanted next." They all said they wanted someone to help them use the tool in their organization. This led us to build our online courses, coaching modules, and enterprise solutions for larger organizations to assist them to implement these tools into their own organizations."

Both Alan and Strategyzer were rapidly building out an "ecosystem" of products for a variety of customer segments. Some things they would give away for free (their YouTube

channel is rich with training videos and has millions of views);
some products are inexpensive but highly valuable (their books
and online courses may cost anywhere from $40 to a few
thousand dollars); right the way through to highly bespoke
implementation solutions for large enterprises. No one product
or service is more important than the other, they each feed the
ecosystem to make the whole greater than the sum of its parts.

Web: www.strategyzer.com
Amazon: Search "Business Model Generation:
A handbook for visionaries, game changers, and challengers"
and "Value Proposition Design: How to create products and
services customers want"

STEP 4: PROFILE

Key People of Influence are known, liked and trusted in their industry. It doesn't happen by accident; it takes a strategy and focused work to build your profile.

You don't need to build a profile that makes you a household name in order to be seen as a Key Person of Influence, but you do need to become "web-famous" when someone goes looking for you online.

When people Google you, they want to see videos, blogs, photos, and groups you are part of. They want to be able to make friends with you, read your content and see the mutual friends and ideas you share. Nothing is more disappointing than meeting someone who seems interesting, but who doesn't come up in a Google search. It makes people question your value.

Over the past few years, we've come to believe that you are who Google says you are.

YOU HAVE A RICH "MEDIA MOGUL" UNCLE

Imagine that one day you get a letter from your rich uncle who just happens to be a billionaire media mogul. He's devastated that you have been estranged for all these years and he wants to make it up to you. He says that all you need to do is video record yourself and he will distribute it worldwide for you for free on his network. He says that if you record some audio, he will have it available on air all over the world. He says that if you write an article, he will publish it and make it available in all corners of the globe.

What would you do? Would you write back and say, "Sorry, I'm really a bit busy right now. I'm not good with technology and I've never done it before. I'd rather not promote myself to a global audience... but thanks all the same."?

If you are reading this kind of book, I'm sure you would drop everything to take up this great opportunity.

The reality is that someone *is* making these offers to you. There are free opportunities to get your videos, audio, articles, images, and ideas out to the world right now, through social media.

A client of mine is known as "The Posture Doctor." She's a chiropractic doctor who specializes in helping people correct poor posture. She launched a YouTube channel with posture correction advice and was shocked at the massive uptake: in the first year over one million people watched her videos. She focused her effort into a niche, she built a profile online and the opportunities came marching in.

SIX OBJECTIVES FOR BUILDING YOUR PROFILE

I have six clear business outcomes when building a profile both online and offline:

1. GENERATE LEADS AND ENQUIRIES

When you build a profile, sites such as LinkedIn, Twitter, Facebook, Instagram, and SlideShare become powerful tools for generating leads.

Earlier I talked about the need to give away as much as possible for free. Social media allows you to give enormous value to the world for free and it comes back to you in the form of leads. Additionally, a lot of referrals these days happen through social media platforms. After all, generating leads is simply about starting conversations with your target market, and these platforms are now where the global conversation is happening.

2. CONVERT LEADS AND ENQUIRIES INTO SALES

Imagine you go to a website for an accountant. When you get there, you find videos to watch, audio downloads, photos, slides, and blogs to read. Imagine you see a list of publications this business has been featured in and links to the stories.

Is that going to make you more likely to do business with them? It sure is. Without a doubt, the more a potential client sees you're a trusted person already, the more likely they are to buy.

3. INCREASE THE AVERAGE SPEND

When people know more, they buy more. After years in sales and business I have discovered that, when you add it all up, a buyer will spend about seven hours deliberating over a substantial purchase. Whether it is a big TV, a training course, a car, or a vacation, consumers will invest several hours researching before they buy. If that's the case, you want to occupy as much of that seven hours as possible. You want them to be listening to your podcasts, watching your videos, following your Twitter feed, and reading your blogs.

As they do this, they're getting better educated on how much they should be allocating. Normally people start out thinking about getting the cheapest option, but with the right education they see the value in spending money on a higher-quality product.

4. INCREASE THE FREQUENCY OF PURCHASING

In this busy world, people can simply forget about you. But not if they read your blogs, see your Facebook updates, follow your Twitter feed, and subscribe to your YouTube channel. Keeping people up-to-date results in more purchases per client per year. If you email people every week they will unsubscribe and feel pestered by you. If they subscribe to your social media profiles, they look forward to your updates.

5. REDUCE COSTS

A strong profile saves you a fortune in the cost associated with chasing business. You'll reduce your marketing, printing, communications, and customer service costs for a start.

Without a profile, you might end up advertising to readers who aren't remotely interested in what you offer; you end up paying for a lot of "eyeballs" that just don't care.

6. IMPROVE YOUR OVERALL BRAND

A consistent message that is all over the internet is a valuable thing when it comes time to making sales, raising investment, or selling your business. It's also great for your team to see, as well as suppliers and joint venture partners.

If ever you are criticized publicly, it helps to have built up a strong reputation to put any critique into a broader context.

BECOMING "GOOGLE-ABLE"

When you Google search a Key Person of Influence, it's clear who they are, what they look like (photos and videos), what they have to say, and how to get in touch with them.

It's not difficult to pass the Google test if you embrace social media because Google will rank information on these main websites highly. You must have a rich library of blogs, videos, slide decks, and images on sites like YouTube, LinkedIn, Instagram, Facebook, SlideShare, and Twitter.

Google will love you if you have a presence on these websites and you take some time each month to keep your profiles up to date. You'll begin to see people coming your way when they search for your name or keywords it finds in your profiles.

Your followers, friends, and fans will love you too, because they quickly get to know you through your videos, photos, groups, and articles.

It's important to remember, however, that your success online can only be as good as your perfect pitch. If your message isn't strong, you'll be wasting your time, or worse, you might even be damaging your brand.

Remember, social media is like a microphone that amplifies you out to every corner of the world. Most people are too busy playing with the technology and go off-message.

DON'T SEEK THE SPOTLIGHT, *BE* THE SPOTLIGHT

You might think that to be a Key Person of Influence you need to be an extraverted, charismatic showman. The person who is always in front of camera, talking on stage, or flashing their Rolex.

This couldn't be further from the truth.

I know a lot of great entrepreneurs who would describe themselves as introverted. In fact, they would consider themselves to be quiet, reserved, and in some cases even a little shy in nature.

Yet when it comes to talking about their business, they speak with authority. They're excited about the trends they're noticing in their industry. They're quick to mention examples and case studies of their clients' results. They speak about their ideas, philosophies, and methods with grounded enthusiasm and passion.

You won't see Warren Buffett or Bill Gates in the media talking about how great Warren Buffett or Bill Gates are (despite their extraordinary achievements). Instead, they're pitching their vision for a different, better world. They're publishing their ideas, writing papers, and appearing in media to share what insights they've discovered in their field.

As Key People of Influence, they aren't stepping into the spotlight. They *are* the spotlight.

In contrast, you can smell a shameless self-promoter from a mile away. They have an agenda and you can easily tell it's all about them. They talk a big talk, but when pressed for their client case studies, results, or proof they go quiet. Their personal brand and positioning in the market is more smoke and mirrors than backed up by a credible track record or case studies.

If you're good at what you do, let your results speak for themselves. Let your ideas carry their own weight online. It's time to start creating the content, collateral, and digital assets that showcase the results you've already achieved. Your authority within your niche will naturally flow as a consequence of this, not because you tried to "build a personal brand" through self-promotion.

THE BEST IS YET TO COME

Whatever you do, don't worry that you might have missed the boat on this new technology. It's just getting started.

The first ten years of social media was simply platform building and people were just using it for the fun of it. We will not see the full effects unfold for many years into the future.

I remember my grandmother telling me about the excitement

she felt about a new railway line that connected her up to a big city when she was a teenager.

Realistically, though, it wasn't the train or the tracks that was so exciting. The new railway line meant she was able to access a whole new world of possibility faster than ever before. New people, new ideas, new resources, and new inspiration.

She wasn't the only one who saw the possibilities. After railway lines, highways, phones, and air travel connected people in the first fifty years of the 1900s, a global boom in creativity occurred.

By giving designers, engineers, entrepreneurs, investors, and entertainers access to new markets, the world saw new music, entertainment, medicine, technology, and products unfold to an unprecedented degree.

It is the same story throughout history. Before every boom in creativity comes a new way to connect—coaches, cars, phones, trains, planes. When humans can connect fast, we can create fast.

I predict a creative boom in art, entertainment, medicine, architecture, fashion, technology, and many other industries that we can barely comprehend right now. In every one of these fields there will be hundreds of micro-niches, and in each little niche there will be Key People of Influence.

Building your profile online and offline will tap you into these trends as they unfold. A great wave of innovation is happening; if you become known, liked, and trusted, you'll be surfing the wave rather than being swept out to sea.

After building a profile, the real trick is for Key People of Influence to connect in meaningful ways. KPIs need to connect with the right people and do deals that raise the value of everyone involved.

The next step is about partnership and it's often called the "money step." When you are ready to see how to make all your work pay off, turn the page for the final step in the KPI Method.

BONUSES

To learn more about building your profile as a Key Person of Influence, join an upcoming workshop here: www.kpiwebclass.com

While you're online, connect with **Mike Reid, our Canadian CEO:**

www.linkedin.com/in/mikejamesreid
www.facebook.com/mikejamesreid.ca
www.instagram.com/mikejamesreid
www.mikejamesreid.com

CASE STUDY: RACHEL DAVID,
FOUNDER OF HASHTAG COMMUNICATIONS

I first met Rachel David at an industry event with some of Toronto's most influential entrepreneurs.

Rachel is the founder of Hashtag Communications, a leading influencer marketing company based out of Toronto. She and her team specialize in running influencer marketing campaigns for some of Canada's largest brands, like RBC, Best Buy, Google, Manulife, and Bell.

What's fascinating about Rachel's story is her company has only been running for three years. Yet, in a short space of time, she's widely become known as one of the "go-to" people for influencer marketing in Canada. How did that come about?

When I sat down with Rachel and asked her what helped establish her brand so quickly, she replied:

> "Being a practitioner of what I preach, I started making my own content that was authentic to me and what I was going through (building and running a company) and it quickly positioned myself as a thought leader in the space."

Rachel has been in the TV and media industry for most of her professional career and she understands what the power of a strong message delivered through the right channels can do.

Since 2015 Rachel has been documenting her life journey on platforms like YouTube and LinkedIn. In a short space of time her videos have amassed millions of views and tens of thousands of subscribers. Rachel talks about all kinds of topics from dating to career decisions to networking tips and how to monetize your brand.

You see, often I talk with small business owners who realize they need to be sharing their message with the world but they don't know what to say. They get so paralysed trying to figure out what to say and how to say it they miss the opportunity before them.

The truth of the matter is, people buy from people. For someone to get "bought into you," they want to get to know, like, and trust you. The best way to do that is to document your journey, what you're passionate about and the things you talk about daily in your business and life.

As Rachel says, both her and the biggest brands in the world know that for their message to stand out:

> "You need to communicate from a very pure place and really identify what you want to contribute to the world (how you will add value) before pressing the record button."

Behind every great influential leader is a system for how they share their message at scale. After years of being a content creator, Rachel has refined a systematic way she can maintain an online brand while also maintaining a life. She has a highly engaged audience of over 70,000 people following her across social media, while also running a fast-growth company servicing clients all over North America.

Rachel was invited to do her first TEDx Vancouver talk in 2019 on "How influencers have transformed modern marketing." All these things have resulted in her becoming a sought-after speaker and commentator in her field, dramatically increasing her inbound leads and opportunities. By harnessing the power of the 5P's, Rachel has become a Key Person of Influence in her industry all before the age of 30 years old.

YouTube: www.youtube.com/racheldavid
Web: www.hashtagcommunications.ca

CASE STUDY: PHILLIP HAID, FOUNDER OF PUBLIC INC.

Phillip Haid is a man on a mission.

When I sat down with him in his sprawling office on the east side of downtown Toronto, it was clear to see he was already having an enormous impact with his business (although Phil would say he's only just getting started).

Phillip is the co-founder of PUBLIC Inc., a full-service strategy and marketing agency transforming the ways in which brands can profit with purpose. Operating since 2008, PUBLIC Inc. has close to forty staff (as of the date of publishing) and has worked with some of Canada's and the world's most recognized brands, including TD Bank, Rexall, The Body Shop, Converse, Rogers, Johnson & Johnson, and Tiffany & Co., just to name a few.

At the core of PUBLIC Inc.'s mission is the thesis that companies can be major creators of positive social impact and also make healthy profits along the way. Large enterprises of the 20th century have primarily demonstrated that profit exists in conjunction with devastating costs to our natural resources, people, and the planet.

Today PUBLIC Inc. exists to prove that in the 21st century, integrating business benefit and community benefit is a mutually reinforcing and scalable proposition. That, in fact, community benefit becomes an explicit goal of enterprise, and society's needs and challenges are factored into mainstream business decisions, not as an afterthought. This is what Phillip calls "profit with purpose," and Phillip believes it is the future of business.

How did Phil create such traction with his business?

Well, it all starts with a compelling vision and an ability to articulate that clearly through a pitch. When someone asks him, "What do you do?" he has a powerful answer that delivers clarity, audience curiosity, and a clear mission.

Phil also writes for and shares his thought leadership in well-recognized publications like *Huffington Post*, *Fast Company* and the *Financial Post* on cause marketing and how companies can profit through social purpose.

When you Google "Phillip Haid," he has a highly credible profile and dominates the first page of Google with links to his company, the publications he's written in and websites where he and his company has been profiled, like Bloomberg.

When Phil expanded PUBLIC Inc.'s operations into the US, he did so through a local partner on the ground in New York City. When I asked Phil about his philosophy and approach to partnerships, he replied:

> "Partnerships have gone to the heart of how we've approached scaling. When we look for partners, we're looking for people and companies that we share a similar market with, but do different things. It's then just figuring out how we can collaborate, share resources, and both grow as a result."

On all accounts, Phillip has been leveraging the five skills of a Key Person of Influence to establish his personal brand in his field, helping build PUBLIC Inc. into one of North America's leading and most well-established cause marketing agencies.

LinkedIn: www.linkedin.com/in/philhaid
Web: https://publicinc.com

STEP 5: PARTNERSHIP

What I am about to share with you is the secret that separates the KPIs who make real money from the people who look good but still don't make the sort of money they are worth.

The key is partnerships. This is where you get to multiply time and rapidly achieve extraordinary results by working with other Key People of Influence.

Consider that someone has already built a relationship with thousands of people who could be your clients. That list is on someone's hard drive right now.

Someone already has free products they would happily add to your product range just for the exposure. Those products are ready to ship in a warehouse right now.

Someone already has a great brand and is looking for worthy products to endorse. They are already more famous than you ever plan to be.

Just as you have worked hard in the last five years to create your pieces of the puzzle, someone else has worked just as hard and is holding onto the missing piece that you need. When the two of you connect up, the money can flow at an alarming rate.

When I was growing our business in Australia, in the very early days we didn't have a strong brand presence or much traction in the market. What we did have were some powerful ideas that we knew more people should know about and a drive to find ways to collaborate with the local small business community to spread them.

At the time, we committed to running a big event for entrepreneurs, set a date four months away, booked a venue, and started hitting the phones. My partners and I cold called hundreds of small businesses and pitched them on what our company did and that we were running an event with 500 entrepreneurs in three months.

Of course, at the time we didn't have anyone attending or a large email list of our own to market to—that's why we needed to partner with those who already did.

We decided to invite these businesses and influential entrepreneurs to a series of dinners to find ways to collaborate. We went along with collateral, slide decks, and a well-tuned pitch talking about ways we could add value to their business by being a partner at the upcoming conference. By the time we'd finished explaining what we wanted to do to support our partners, they were so excited they were asking us how they could help promote the event.

The dinners, printing, and running the event cost us $40,000, of which only $20,000 needed to be paid up front. We ended up making over $500,000 in new sales revenue in the five days following that event.

Rather than running expensive advertising campaigns, I focused on engaging with Key People of Influence and creating win/win partnerships. It resulted in a very lucrative start to doing business in Australia.

THE SPIRIT OF PARTNERSHIP

When I think about partnerships, it starts with the right spirit of intent. You can't fake it when it comes to a successful partnership: you genuinely have to care about the wants and desires of the person you're doing the deal with. You need to see it from their side of the table and work as hard for them as you want them to work for you—or even more so.

This starts with your internal team of people who work with you every day. The spirit of partnership has to begin at the core of your business with the co-founders, the employees, and the suppliers.

Even the way you view those around you sets the tone for partnership. Richard Branson describes the Virgin employees as the "team." He uses that word because he genuinely recognizes that he is only able to achieve his goals through partnering with others.

Beyond the internal team, the external relationships also thrive when there's a spirit of partnership. Your customers and clients are in partnership with your business in a way—they want a result and you want their business; if you focus on their needs, they will take care of yours.

Your investor relationships will only last if you see them as your partners. Their money is allowing you to speed up your growth and your operation is providing them with a return on capital. It can be easy for an entrepreneur to forget how important that first investment was after the business is making big profits, and investors sometimes forget that they were the ones who backed your long-term plan. With the spirit of partnership the relationship works.

Don't try to squeeze every drop out of a relationship. Allow others to have their triumphs, celebrate the wins of others even if it's not yet your turn. All of it comes down to being a good partner and being a good partner ensures you are a Key Person of Influence for the long run.

THE TOOLS

Without the spirit of partnership, the tools are fairly useless, but provided you're creating win/win relationships you'll need a few ways to manage them.

NEGOTIATIONS

It's worthwhile learning the art and science of negotiations. The way you present a deal has a huge impact on the way it is received. The wording you use, the meeting place, the materials you bring and the way you follow up all impact the quality of the partnerships you form.

I do not believe you should use negotiation tactics to create unfair agreements; they simply won't last. I do believe that you should approach all negotiations in a professional way so that you reach an outcome you are happy with and your partners are happy too. Good negotiations never involve manipulation; good negotiation skills revolve around your ability to see the full picture from both sides of the negotiation. It requires both parties to make sacrifices for the good of the partnership long-term.

WRITTEN AGREEMENTS

Key People of Influence often attract many partners and a lot gets discussed. In the spirit of good partnership, it's worth making sure that you keep a written agreement of any partnerships you create. This could be an employment contract, it could be an email confirmation, a Heads of Terms agreement, or a fully developed contract put together by a law firm. Regardless of the way you choose to document the agreement, do it for the best interests of everyone involved, not so you can enforce a carefully concealed clause.

SYSTEMS

There are systems that track where every sale came from and pay a commission to the person who helped generate that sale. These are perfect for scaling marketing and referral agreements.

There are systems that measure how much time each contractor, supplier, or employee puts into a project. There are systems for managing a crowd-funded shareholding with multiple investors.

Without these sorts of systems you simply can't scale your partnerships. You want to invest in systems that allow you to have clear, clean relationships with people all over the world.

WHAT KIND OF DEALS CAN YOU START WITH?

There are several types of deals that I recommend you do as you build your skills as a Key Person of Influence.

AFFILIATE PARTNERSHIPS

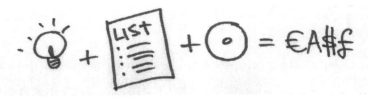

This is a partnership that encourages people to promote your products in exchange for a commission. The system uses tracking codes and links to report where every sale originated from and with the right software you can manage thousands of affiliates who all promote you and promptly receive a commission when they generate a sale.

It's not a new concept (professionals have been paying finder's fees for years), but with modern technology you can really ramp it up.

Imagine you launch a website selling t-shirts for $50. The front of the site is a normal-looking store, but there's also a back-end portal for affiliates.

When an affiliate logs into the site, they are given a special link. They are told that anyone who arrives at the site through this link, and buys a t-shirt, will be logged as their affiliate sale and a commission of 20% will be paid.

As an affiliate they are free to use email, Twitter, Facebook, blogs, or videos to promote your site. The more people who click the link and buy a t-shirt, the more money they make and so do you. The power of this system is that you don't spend your marketing money until after the sale is made.

We run Key Person of Influence events around the world and rather than spending a fortune on advertising up front, we engage with local supporters and run a grass-roots affiliate campaign. After we've run the event the commissions are paid or rewards are issued.

You can register your interest in being an affiliate by emailing mike@dent.global with "Partnerships" in the subject line.

CO-PROMOTION

This is when two companies with similar-sized databases each email or post to their audiences about the other's offer.

Sometimes the audiences aren't exactly the same size, so you need to agree on how you will get around this. One company might add some money into the deal or mail their list several times to make up the difference.

You will quickly discover that some of the people who never respond to your offers are suddenly interested in the new product you offer as part of the mail swap.

PRODUCT CREATION PARTNERSHIPS

This is where you team up with another person or a group to create a more valuable new product.

Imagine a personal trainer teams up with an image consultant and a photographer to create a "Complete Makeover" package. It's a great way for all three businesses to work together and help the client to get the best result possible.

Always approach this with the question: "What is my client trying to accomplish when they work with me, and who could I team up with to get us an even better outcome?"

In the above example, the client isn't looking to lift heavy plates of metal, spend money on clothes, or sit around smiling at a cameraman. They want to tone up, look fashionable, and get some great photos while they are looking their best.

By thinking about how you can help your client "get something done," you will be able to identify who can help you to help your client.

PACKAGING UP

This is very similar to Product Teaming, except you are looking to add someone else's existing products to your own existing products. Imagine you are a restaurant and you are next to a cinema. You could do a "Movie-Meal Deal" and capture more customers and extra revenue.

Think about the existing products and services that would complement your own product nicely and create a bundle.

FREE-BUNDLE GROUP

Everyone likes free stuff. Even better, they love bundles of free stuff. Why not team up with several businesses to put together an irresistible "basket of free goodies."

Let's imagine that you have a free meditation class that you offer to potential clients, while the yoga studio down the road gives away a free first lesson, and a chiropractor friend gives away a free spine assessment. If you do a joint venture (JV), each of you now has a very nice free offer you can use to attract new business and promote each other's businesses.

How easy would it be to generate new leads if you created a free bundle worth hundreds?

GETTING STARTED WITH PARTNERSHIPS

All the time I hear people say, "I just had a good idea but how do I actually make it happen?"

Firstly, you should never ask, *"How* do I make it happen?" You should ask, *"Who* do I need to talk to?"

Whenever you have an idea, no matter how crazy, make at least three calls to see if it's possible.

Making three calls can yield you some amazing results.

You're typically missing either a strong brand, the right product, or distribution of message in scaling your business. In the example earlier in this chapter, I had a hot product (an event with 500 entrepreneurs) but needed powerful brands to associate with and distribution of message to promote the event.

Think about the "missing link" you have in your business right now and write a list of three people you could call to see if you could provide some of what you have in exchange for some of what they've got that you're missing.

GO NETWORKING FOR PARTNERSHIPS—NOT CLIENTS

One of the key differences between Key People of Influence and everyone else is that KPIs don't go out looking for clients, they go looking for partnerships.

Going out to a networking event looking for a client is like trying to get to China on foot. If you want to go to China, you don't want to go one step at a time, you want to figure out who already flies there in a jet.

KPIs only go networking to find leverage. They are looking for people who have a big database of clients, a channel of distribution, a great brand, an awesome product, or some other key aspect of value or leverage.

I often get frustrated when people come up to me at a networking function and try to get me to become a client. I almost always like it when someone is thinking about a mutually beneficial partnership.

To step things up as a Key Person of Influence, forget looking for clients and start looking for relationships that can benefit both parties. Your job is to discover:

- People who have a list of potential clients.
- People interested in co-producing something.
- People with products that could be attractive to your contact list.
- People who would make valuable additions to your team.
- People who could be beneficial contacts for someone you know.

This will yield better results than going around thinking, "Can I make a sale right here and now?"

ANYTHING IS POSSIBLE WITH THE RIGHT PARTNERS

A radical idea becomes plausible when you have the right partners. If someone tells me they want to attract 100,000 customers I will probably have my doubts. If they then explain that they have partnerships with major media companies, celebrities, retail outlets, and investors, I might start to think, "only 100,000?"

Few things can happen when you work in isolation; with the right partners anything is possible.

Whenever you want to take your income to a higher level, go looking for a higher-level partnership and meet them to discuss a deal that works for everyone.

MEETING A POTENTIAL PARTNER

It can be nerve-racking sitting down with someone who has the power to double your quarterly sales with a single email. You want to make sure you get a few things right so that the deal goes ahead and the relationship is long lasting.

SET THE SCENE

I always meet people in either a private members' club or a nice restaurant. I don't meet people in my office or theirs because the spirit of a partnership should be about meeting on common ground to create a win/win/win (you win, they win, the customer wins) deal. It creates the wrong starting point if one person has to make the trip to the other person's office. I also like meeting in nice locations because a JV or partnership should be about creating wealth and abundance for everyone involved.

BRING A GIFT

When I meet with a potential partner I like to bring a thoughtful gift to show that I am thinking of their needs. It might be a copy of a book I would recommend for them or even something simple like a magazine article clipping I think they might be interested in. It's not to demonstrate that I am spending a lot of money on them, it's to demonstrate that I am already thinking about their interests.

MAKE FRIENDS FIRST

A deal will not normally happen if you don't like each other, even if the deal is perfect in every other way. Conversely, if you do like each other you will find it easy to make a deal work.

I normally talk about anything other than business until I am sure I like the person and they like me. I don't do this as a trick or to win favour, I genuinely want to do business with people I like and share common ground with.

DO BUSINESS LAST

When you know you have rapport and it seems entirely appropriate to bring up business, it should only take 15–20 minutes to make a deal work at a top-line level. Much longer than that and it might not be a good deal to be doing.

Always go into a meeting with a fair deal in mind and know in advance what you are flexible on and where you can't budge.

PICK UP THE BILL

I am personally a fan of genuinely offering to pick up the bill, especially if I instigated the meeting. For me it shows that I valued the meeting with them. Of course, if they insist on splitting the bill

I am ok with it, because it shows we are both thinking 50–50 even on small things.

FOLLOW THROUGH

After a meeting, allow ten to fifteen minutes to follow through on anything you mentioned you would do. Sometime in the course of the conversation you might say that you will email through a website address or a name of a book, or connect two people on email.

Very few people actually follow through on these off-hand remarks, but it gets noticed when you do follow through and it sends a powerful message that what you say and what you do are the same thing.

EXPECT MAGIC

The most rewarding part of building a business with the spirit of partnership in everything you do is the unexpected rewards that show up.

You know you've built solid partnerships when you're constantly surprised by how things turn out better than you expected.

Great partnerships have allowed me to make progress in ways I would have never imagined. As a result of partnerships I've seen my businesses go global, I've received investment at the valuation I wanted, I have earned a high income, I've been given shares in growth companies, I have had a lot of fun, been invited on unique trips away, and met my entrepreneurial heroes.

None of these things would have happened if I hadn't built strong relationships that turned into strong partnerships.

EXERCISES

What three calls can you make right now?

- Three people who already have a list?
- Three businesses that give away free stuff for your bundle?
- Three people who you can team up with and make a product?

What three calls could you make (regardless of how scary) that could really get your ideas off the ground?

Go for it!

ACTION STEP

For additional content relating to this step visit:
https://ca.dent.global/partnership/

NOTES ...

CASE STUDY: TODD HERMAN, AUTHOR OF THE ALTER EGO EFFECT AND FOUNDER OF 90 DAY YEAR

Todd Herman lives, breathes, and sweats peak performance, which is to be expected from a man who has been working with elite athletes (amateur, pro, Olympians), entrepreneurs, and executives for the last twenty years to help them achieve extraordinary levels of performance in their sport or careers. He does this by giving them proven mental game strategies to help calm nerves, compete confidently, and ultimately win more.

When I first heard Todd talk at an industry event in Toronto, I knew this man was a master of his craft. Not only that, I instantly knew he was a master of the five principles of a Key Person of Influence as well.

Todd opened the talk with a conversation structure I was all too familiar with. He gave his audience immediate clarity on the domain he was a specialist in, established why he was credible enough to talk on that topic, and helped connect us to the problems most people face in reaching higher levels of flow state for superhuman creativity, output, and performance.

As he shared stories from his recent best-selling book *The Alter Ego Effect: The power of secret identities to transform your life*, the audience was hanging on to every word. Todd is, of course, a highly engaging speaker, but when I asked him how often he had shared those same stories before he replied:

> "Hundreds and hundreds of times. I'm constantly toiling away at my choice of words so the message gets communicated in a powerful way for my audience."

Todd's stories, methods, and frameworks for how he delivers such transformative results to his clients have been refined over decades of practice and work. Unfortunately, many entrepreneurs struggle to expand their influence because they keep their methods to themselves and don't package them so they can share them with the world more broadly. Not so in Todd's case.

Writing the book *The Alter Ego Effect* gave his ideas a vessel that could spread much farther and wider. While we all have the tools to publish at our fingertips, publishing a hard-copy book remains one of the most credible and powerful ways to get those ideas to spread. They open doors in ways you couldn't imagine. As Todd explains:

> "It's a funny thing. I've had a great career for the past 22 years before the book and have a solid Rolodex of leaders from many industries. But the moment the book came out and then hit bestseller lists, my personal brand and value increased immediately. There's just a different perception of a published author, and the floodgates of speaking engagements [have] been opened more widely now."

Todd has also formalized his methods and peak performance systems into a program he calls the "90 Day Year" that is helping entrepreneurs around the world gain the clarity, focus, and structure required to grow and scale their businesses—without wasting effort on projects that won't move the needle.

When you Google "Todd Herman" a raft of videos, podcasts, and articles show up all reinforcing that Todd is the expert in his field. He's built a formidable following on his own social media accounts of more than 100,000 followers. He's regularly invited as a keynote speaker to share his insights and has featured on Sky Business News, *The Today Show*, PBS, CBS Sports, the *NY Times*, CBS Radio, *Huffington Post*, and Business Insider.

Because of his profile, other Key People of Influence in Todd's field and adjacent fields want to find ways to work and collaborate with him. Thanks to the domino effect of everything Todd has put in place, he has a powerful network right at his fingertips. Ultimately, like all Key People of Influence, Todd has the leverage to curate his own opportunities—not chase them.

Todd is another Canadian entrepreneur who is making waves in his industry by packaging his value for scale and establishing himself as a visible leader in his field.

LinkedIn: www.linkedin.com/in/toddherman1
Web: https://toddherman.me
Amazon: Search "The Alter Ego Effect: The power of secret identities to transform your life"

SIMPLE AND POWERFUL... BUT WILL YOU SUCCEED?

What I have shared with you may seem simple. I've given you just five things to focus on. Never underestimate the power of simplicity.

You'll start to see this formula everywhere now you know it. You'll see top entrepreneurs, highly paid CEOs, politicians, athletes, and celebrities using these five strengths.

In-built into these five outcomes for becoming a Key Person of Influence, you will find that there is clarity, credibility, visibility, scalability, and profitability.

Over the next twelve months I can guarantee you that my inbox will be full of people emailing me their success stories as a result of following this method.

I already know what they will say. Their emails will tell me that they did the work, pushed through their limiting beliefs, made the time and did all five of the steps in order. They will then tell me that just as I had promised, opportunities started to come their way, more money began to flow and they started to have more fun.

They will tell me that they experienced three big benefits after doing the work set out in this book:

1. They earn more money with less stress and struggle.
2. They enjoy greater status and recognition in their industry and have more fun.
3. They attract more opportunities that are right for them.

I sincerely want *you* to be in that group. I want your story in my inbox, telling me that you have done these five simple things, made yourself an opportunity magnet, earned more money, had more fun, and created more success.

Sadly, there's a good chance you won't be. People can get addicted to the struggle and let complexity get in the way of simplicity; let the unimportant stuff replace the most important stuff; or worse, let the desire for immediate quick wins creep in.

Over the last ten years, I have studied people's decision-making habits like a hawk. As a marketing person, I am insatiably interested in human behaviour and watching how people make decisions and take action for their businesses and their lives.

In the next few chapters I will share with you some of the things I have noticed when watching highly successful people make decisions, versus people who are perpetually frozen in the headlights of life.

The next chapters will offer some ideas on how you can overcome the obstacles and become the Key Person of Influence in your chosen field faster and without as many struggles.

3

MAKING IT HAPPEN

Our daily routines, habits, and traditional education has gotten us this far; however, now they are holding us back.

We need to overcome the obstacles that get in the way of becoming a Key Person of Influence.

It is not enough to know the path; we must walk it.

NEWCOMERS, WORKER-BEES, AND KPIS

There's a predictable journey you'll go on as you pursue success, achievement, and influence. Every industry has three layers of people—newcomers, worker-bees, and Key People of Influence.

The newcomers are enthusiastic, excited, and full of dreams. They believe that this new industry they are in will fulfill their dreams and take them places. Newcomers are normally willing to work hard for little pay in the short term in the belief that the rewards will come later. Typically, they have seen the results that a KPI has achieved and they want to replicate similar success for themselves.

The worker-bees are the people in the industry who are doing the work but not getting ahead. Some of their previous dreams have been knocked out of them. When they were newcomers, they thought that their industry would be fresh, new, exciting, and rewarding. Now it seems a bit stale and they are secretly resentful of the Key People of Influence (for their effortless results) and the newcomers (for their spark and enthusiasm). The worker-bees at some point may have enjoyed the work, but are often disappointed that the results aren't coming in fast enough.

As we now know, the Key People of Influence make it look easy. They always have lots of opportunity flowing around them and they achieve great results quickly. Their email inbox is full of people trying to get good opportunities to them. With a few phone calls they can make magic happen and get some of the spoils.

They also attract lots of newcomers into their industry because they make success seem so easy.

THE MERRY-GO-ROUND OF DISTRACTION

This dynamic causes a strange phenomenon. Jaded worker-bees go buzzing about new industries and they spy a Key Person of Influence in that new area. They get excited and decide to become a newcomer to that industry. They feel the rush and the excitement that comes with a brand-new project. They see how effortlessly success comes to the KPIs in that industry. Even if a worker-bee enjoyed their previous job, they think to themselves, "I like what I do, but I don't get the rewards, so if I can make easy money in this new field, I can always go back to what I do and not worry about the money."

Like most newcomers they get energized and do lots of work for little rewards. They expect that this work will pay off this time in the long run.

After a while, the newcomer gets a bit tired and it feels like hard work with less of the spark. They have now met many worker-bees in this new industry who say things like, "It's hard work in this industry; I've been at it for years and I still haven't seen the big rewards yet."

The newcomer becomes a worker-bee and eventually begins looking around for the next big thing that will provide an easy win. As this continues, they get further and further from pursuing their passion by constantly chasing the next easy win.

This opportunistic behaviour is the very thing that prevents opportunities from flowing.

The answer to this conundrum is simple. You must focus on your passion and become a Key Person of Influence in that field. As soon as you are a KPI you will not even notice opportunities in other industries because you will be swamped with great things to do in your own industry. And the rewards will come thick and fast.

There's no easy money, no quick wins, and no big payoff for newcomers or worker-bees. Not in property, not in shares, not on the internet, not in a franchise, not in a network marketing business, not in technology, software, FOREX, wearables, apps, or e-commerce. Easy wins go to Key People of Influence. Period.

Resist the temptation to chase the new thing and keep taking steps closer to the inner circle of the industry you love. Stop looking elsewhere and focus on implementing the KPI Method. When you focus on the five steps in this book and arrive as a Key Person of Influence, you will get to be the "overnight success" others are talking about.

IGNORE THE COMPETITION

Much in the same way the merry-go-round of distraction leads people to abandon the industry they're passionate about, focusing on the competition in the industry you do love can be equally damaging.

The truth is, every industry is competitive. They all go through a predictable life cycle:

A new technology is developed or some new value is created. Entrepreneurs who spot the trend become early innovators and capitalize on an under-served market. Eventually the industry matures until there is lots of competition and profits are scarce for every entrepreneur other than the Key People of Influence.

Focusing on the competition leads to converging toward mediocrity. Without even realizing it you begin to watch and mimic everything your competition says or does. An outsider looking in can't see the difference between you and everyone else.

If you constantly focus on the competition, you are destined to blend into a sea of sameness.

Key People of Influence are constantly producing more work, having fresh ideas, spotting new trends, and developing new insights. They focus on staying relevant and as a result stay at the top of their game.

WHO HAS FREEDOM?

I often get asked the question: "If I become a Key Person of Influence, won't that mean I get trapped in my business and I won't be able to ever take a vacation, move abroad, or sell my business?"

It seems logical that a person who has a profile and is seen to be the driving force of a business would be trapped in the business, but in practical terms nothing is further from the truth.

Key People of Influence have far more freedom for several reasons.

Firstly, they attract talent. Highly skilled and talented people don't want to work with just anyone; they want to work with KPIs. When you position yourself as a KPI, you'll start to see brilliant people who show up and make remarkable things happen. These people will be autonomous, value-focused people who start to grow your business in all directions whether you're in the room or not. Pretty soon you'll have so much talent buzzing around your enterprise that there will seem to be a steady stream of savvy people always showing up. This is called "high-performance culture" and it's a big asset, whether you want to sell your business one day or hand over the day-to-day management to a leader who's better suited to the task than you yourself.

Secondly, people who are KPIs have created assets that deliver value when they aren't even in the room. Richard Branson can be kitesurfing on the beach of his private island and still be having an impact on thousands of people worldwide. He does this through his clear message, his books and articles, his products and services, his profile, and his partnerships. On your own scale, you'll be doing this too as a KPI—even when you're not in the room your presence is felt.

Thirdly, Key People of Influence attract investors, unlike worker-bees. An investor wants to put their money behind the person who's leading the way and going places. A Key Person of Influence can show all the signs that they are worthy of receiving these funds. If there is an exit whereby someone wants to buy the whole company, there are still dozens of options on how you can transfer your brand value to the new owner.

The truth is, nothing is more restrictive than being average and ordinary. The worker-bees in any industry aren't able to get traction or attraction for their ideas.

When Daniel wrote the first edition of the *Key Person of Influence* book in 2010 and released it in the UK, it was merely a concept. Over the next year he proved the concept until Mike and another co-founder expanded the concept in Australia. Now the seed of the business had been germinated, more and more talented people inspired by the vision joined the crusade.

Daniel visited Australia a handful of times in the first few years but largely stayed in the UK. Within a few short years Mike and his partners had built Dent into a top-100 fastest-growing company in Australia.

What we discovered was that people buy into your ideas and ability to solve their problems in a remarkable way. The more we developed the assets that helped them do that, the less they cared who was the original creator of the idea.

Strangely, the more you become a Key Person of Influence in the way we've set out in this book, the less your business relies on you as the Key Person of Influence.

YOU CAN'T DO IT ALONE

There's no such thing as a self-made millionaire; success is always a team sport.

In the previous section we explored the leverage that comes from partnering with others. It saves you years and a lot of money to find the right people to work with.

Well, it doesn't end there. The same principle holds true when it comes to the peer group you surround yourself with, the consequences you're accountable for, and the mentors who guide you.

I am always surprised when someone tries to do something on their own; I'm convinced that some people want to create an "original mistake." In these globally-connected times, you must find an individual or a group of people who already achieved what you want to achieve and learn from them.

When left alone, most people become distracted, bored, discouraged, and uninspired; they will not complete any of the KPI Method outcomes to their full potential. It's almost a cliché that people are "working on a book" yet can let countless hours of great content slip through their fingers.

The truth is we will never achieve our full potential on our own. That's why every great sports personality has a coach; that's why the president has advisers and why great actors have a director to bring out their best.

WOULD YOU EXPECT TO WIN A GAME OF HOCKEY, PLAYING SOLO?

Imagine I told you I'm playing a game of ice hockey against a local team this weekend and explained it's just me against their entire team.

I say, "Well I know it's just me for now, but when I score a goal or two, I'll then start finding people to join my team."

How do you think I'll do?

Clearly, I'm going to lose. I could be the best individual player in the league, but without a team I won't score. The game just doesn't work that way.

Unfortunately, I meet countless business owners who are trying to run their business without a team. They might be new to business or they've had a team in the past, gotten burned with HR issues, and swore never to hire people again.

We talked about being part of a high-performing peer group in the previous section to achieve success. Similarly, it's virtually impossible to achieve both the income and lifestyle freedom most entrepreneurs want without a core team.

When I launched our office for Dent in Brisbane, Australia, one of the first things I did (before any revenue was coming in the door) was source and hire an events manager, appointment setter, and PA. Once I had my core team in place, I could then go out and forage for the first few customers that would get us up and running. With the team in place, I could very quickly scale revenue to meet those new obligations. I started with less than $30,000 in capital.

Within twelve months this division of the business was on a run rate of $80,000 per month and a new leader was put in place to continue its growth.

Without the team I would have been juggling all those responsibilities. Calling all the leads, booking appointments, making sales, calling venues, managing my calendar, and doing all the marketing. It's impossible to wear all those hats and grow a business effectively—even from the beginning.

I've used this exact same formula to launch Dent into Canada. Before we had a more than a handful of customers I had sourced the team I would need to launch. Once they were in place, I could get to work on bringing the first wave of sales in the door to pay the team and scale revenue quickly from there.

Behind every Key Person of Influence is a high-performing, dedicated team that gets stuff done and ultimately makes the KPI look good. This is so a KPI can stick to doing what they do best— pitching for new business, publishing content, building a remarkable product, raising their profile, and connecting with other Key People of Influence as strategic partners.

A great Key Person of Influence knows they need a team as much as a team needs a great KPI.

THE POWER OF CURRENT BEST PRACTICES

Unfortunately, most people who attempt to achieve a breakthrough on their own make costly mistakes. They procrastinate and waste time, and too often they create an inferior product that fails to create the desired outcome. It may even damage their brand rather than build it.

It is disappointing to see someone on video who has nothing unique to say. They talk in general terms and create no depth to their ideas. They were given the gift of having a captive audience, then blew it with amateurism.

Without the right guidance people over-commit to needless expenses (like high-cost printing, design, filming, etc.). They spend their time and money in the wrong area. Nothing really links back to their business model and it all looks a little sad.

People do this because they are unaware of current best practices.

In every industry there are cutting-edge strategies and methods that form the basis of current best practices.

WHAT MAKES THE BEST, THE BEST?

If you look at the profits and losses of some of the largest companies in the world, you will notice they typically spend anywhere from 5–10% of revenues on training and development. What sits behind this number is an attitude toward finding best practices versus experimentation.

As entrepreneurs we naturally like to experiment. We fiercely and independently brave the unknown in pursuit of new growth.

However, I see a lot of entrepreneurs make the mistake of using trial and error as their dominant strategy for building their business. Trial and error has its place, but not at the expense of modelling what already works.

Beyond the obvious hard work and dedication to their craft, if you look to any high performer within any industry you will notice a common thread. They are relentless in modelling the best practices that are already working for what they're looking to achieve.

Find the people and environments that have already demonstrated knowledge or capability in the areas where you're weak.

If you feel you are stubborn or reluctant to seek guidance, then you probably are. The quicker you can let go of that belief, the faster you can apply what Key People of Influence in your industry (or adjacent industries) have already found works.

The most fruitful innovation and experimentation occurs at the fringes and shouldn't account for more than 10–20% of your approach. World-class results are more often than not a function of consistently sticking to what works and not trying to deviate. It's not as glamorous or exciting as constant change, but it's a hell of a lot more profitable.

Start by investing into what's proven, then invest into the unknown.

LEVERAGING EXPERTS

A mentor once said to me, "As soon as you figure out that it's worth paying for great people to work on your business, everything goes to a new level."

Some people who struggle in business hate paying for help. They try to do it all themselves: they try to build their own website, design their own brochures, enter their accounts, and devise their own marketing plans. It's not how the pros do it. People who are high achievers ensure they are surrounded by experts who can help them to implement their vision. They instruct people who know what they are doing and work with them to implement transformation.

They don't risk making painful mistakes that someone else has already made. There are people who have achieved the goals you have set for yourself and they can help you get there faster, cheaper, and at a higher standard.

It's possible to make more money but you can never make more time. If you get the chance to speed up your results, take it—because your time is too precious.

BECOME A BETTER KPI, NOT A BETTER OPERATOR

A great business with under a dozen staff is broadly made up of four core functions: Sales & Marketing, Operations, Finance & Admin, and a Key Person of Influence.

In other words, the functional components of making the business operate are generating leads, making sales, delivering products, managing the money, and general admin.

All of these components are important to making a business successful, but without a strong Key Person of Influence leading from the front, it's very hard to separate this business from any other.

The Key Person of Influence role is the most vital role within your company. It's the role that cannot be easily replicated. It's the role that, when performed well, makes every other function perform better.

When you're a KPI in your industry, it becomes easier for you and your team to make sales. People want to come to your business just so they can connect with you more closely (even if you only show up for a two-hour presentation each week).

Prospects will give more respect to what your team have to say, simply because they respect you as a KPI. They'll pay their bills on time simply because they're doing business with a KPI.

I'll repeat what I said at the start of this book: Key People of Influence attract more opportunities, make more money, and earn more respect simply by virtue of being KPIs in their industry.

Don't get caught thinking that becoming a better operator is the fast-track to more time, money, and freedom. Working with someone like a business coach to create better processes around the functional components of your business can have enormous payoff—but only after you've firmly positioned yourself as a Key Person of Influence. Investing before this will lead to marginal improvements at best and loss of your most precious asset—time.

ILR—THE THREE LETTERS THAT WILL RUIN YOUR LIFE

When I first heard about ILR I was shocked at how many great opportunities I had lost over the years because of this phenomenon.

Cars, business growth, houses, travel, friends, mentors… the list goes on.

It became an obsession to make sure that I dealt with it and got rid of it as best I could.

ILR stands for the Illusion of Limited Resources.

Why would I claim that it is an illusion that resources are limited?

It's not just me saying it. Professor Paul Zane Pilzer, a senior economic adviser and internationally acclaimed author, says that a resource is only defined by our ability to use it. Effectively, there are no resources without resourcefulness. The only reason oil is a resource is because we are resourceful enough to use it for so many things. Before we understood it, it was nothing more than black sludge.

The chances are that you are already standing on an "oil well" of opportunities that are just waiting for you to become resourceful enough to see them.

If you don't believe me, try to imagine what would happen if tomorrow morning Richard Branson swapped lives with you for a year. He would get your house, your car, your friends, your family, your challenges, and even your bank account.

Imagine that he would even have to take on your name and appearance. In twelve months, when you swap back, do you think there would be some noticeable changes in your life?

Of course there would! He would spot opportunities that you had overlooked. He would pick up the phone and have conversations that you would not have had. He would start to introduce himself more powerfully than you currently do.

What about poor Richard Branson when he has to go back to his life a year later? If you hadn't been as resourceful as him, he might find that his island had been repossessed, his planes grounded, his management team had all quit, and his spaceship was missing.

We all want Sir Richard's resources but very few people are willing to get even a little bit more resourceful than they currently are. After reading this book, I sincerely hope you are willing to stretch and do what it takes to become the Key Person of Influence in your industry.

No matter what you need in your business or your life, getting it will be a function of your resourcefulness rather than whether the resources are available. Of course they are available.

The three biggest factors that determine your resourcefulness are:

- The questions you ask.
- The people you know.
- Your willingness to stretch into the unknown.

Let's take a look at these three factors in the next section.

BETTER ANSWERS COME FROM BETTER QUESTIONS

If ever I hear someone complaining about not having access to enough resources, I know to look at the questions they are asking.

When someone gets stuck they are often asking *unresourceful* questions like:

"How come I can't find the time?"

"Why is this so hard?"

"Why can't there just be an easier way?"

"Why do I have to do all this new stuff?"

I know straight away that they need to ask a better question, and immediately they will get a better answer.

Here are some *better* questions:

"Who would absolutely love the chance to work on this project and would be able to do an amazing job?"

"What value can I add to this, that very few people could?"

"How do I make this even better?"

"Who has already achieved the result I want?"

"Who woke up this morning and already has access to the resources I want?"

There's no point complaining and there's no point asking questions that go nowhere. What's a better question you need to ask yourself now?

REQUESTS VERSUS OPPORTUNITIES

By the very fact that you want to grow your business or your levels of influence, you'll need to access resources.

Many people focus on the resources they are lacking and they aren't shy about telling everyone. They attempt to make their problems into someone else's problems. You hear some people say things like:

"I need more sales coming in. Can you help me make more sales?"

"I need my team to get motivated. Can you get me a motivated team?"

"I want more qualified leads. Can someone get me some better leads please?"

All of these are just requests. Unless you are a child asking your parents for something small, the language of requests does not work very often.

Key People of Influence use the language of opportunities. This is where you win, by helping someone else win. When you want something, you express it in a way that works for the person you want assistance from. Here are some examples:

"I need more sales coming in. Would you like to follow up on some hot leads and get 10% of the money you bring in?"

"I need my team to get motivated. If I could see an improvement in performance I would happily share some of the upside with you. What kind of conditions would make that deal a win for you?"

"I want more qualified leads. If we can get more targeted leads, we will save a lot of wasted time and money; I would be happy to share some of those savings with you. Would you like to get involved in that project?"

Great businesspeople speak the language of opportunity *all* the time. In the next week, see if you can eradicate all requests from your language and adopt a policy that you only offer opportunities.

You'll be astonished at how many people will get excited to work with you when there's an opportunity on the table as opposed to a request.

IT'S NOT JUST WHAT YOU KNOW

Given time, a strong network leads to more wealth, more fun, and more success.

Some people go online and "friend" hundreds of people across several social networks. They look at them proudly and marvel at the size of their growing network. In truth, though, they don't have a network; it's a very loose connection at best.

A network is a group of people who share opportunities. You can pick up the phone to them, they happily take your call, and they trust that you will have something valuable to say.

If you think of your network in those terms, how many people do you have in your directory that fit the criteria? How many people do you regularly share opportunities with?

If the number is low, you need to make this a major priority. You will never sustainably increase your wealth without first increasing your network.

The best way to rapidly grow your network is to become part of existing, trusted networks and then show up consistently with a view to be of service.

STRETCHING INTO THE UNKNOWN

Most people believe that when the conditions are right they will act. This attitude does *not* work. Ever.

It's like saying that when all the traffic lights turn green, I will leave my house and drive to work. Not only do the conditions never become perfect for action, but most people become so used to not committing to things that when the time comes for them to act, they just don't do anything.

After witnessing many successful people and many of those who struggle, I can tell you that the people who are successful are the ones who commit to things that take them forward, even when they aren't sure exactly how it will all come together. Those who struggle often describe themselves as "perfectionists," "too busy," or "overly cautious" to mask their inability to take a step into the unknown.

I'm not saying be reckless, I'm saying that there's never a right time. You will *always* have challenges going on with either your time, your money, or your focus. If something comes along that you know you should do, then do it, and figure it out along the way.

PROLIFIC BEATS PERFECT

Another common roadblock for people is the desire to "do it right." In other words, they are afraid of failure, using a well-rationalized form of perfectionism as an excuse.

It might help to remember that anything you ever build or create in your business always goes through a predictable creation to implementation cycle. It starts off as a fuzzy idea, turns into a mess, the mess turns into an experiment, and the experiment turns into something viable or not.

Key People of Influence don't wait for the perfect time; they see an opportunity and they start.

Like weaving a tapestry, they recognize that there will be many threads which don't match or fit in. They're happy about that because when they step back and see the tapestry rapidly unfolding before them, they appreciate its imperfections in the context of the big picture.

The market sees those imperfections, too, but they can't help but admire the beauty of the tapestry as a whole.

Key People of Influence are prolific in producing work and putting it out into the world.

Don't wait to "do it right." Surround yourself with a high-performance peer group and current best practices, and start.

READY, FIRE... AIM!

Here's an example in your hands: this book was written at a time that was incredibly busy for me. If I had decided that in order to write this book I should wait until I had a spare three to four weeks, it would have never happened. Instead, I just started writing it and I committed to write a thousand words a day no matter what.

I have written it on planes, in hotels, and at all hours of the day and night. I even wrote until 4am one night, knowing that I would need to be up at 9:30am. It was difficult to get out of bed, sure, but after a shower I was fine, and I made up the sleep later that afternoon.

I had an accountability group who were checking my progress.

It's funny how much you can achieve if there's a deadline and a group of people watching the process.

Another big example was: when I was twenty-four I wanted to buy myself a BMW X5 with all the extras. Despite knowing exactly what I wanted, I put off the decision for over a year. Then one day a friendly rival of mine bought himself a new BMW. Well that was it: the next day I went down to the finance department and signed up for the lease on the car, not knowing exactly how long I could afford to make my payments. After the lease was approved, it became something I needed to find the money for each month and, sure enough, I did it. It gave me a good reason to get creative and earn more money.

There's no way I would have ever had that car if I had waited until I had "spare" money lying around. That car was a huge source of fun and achievement; to this day I'm really glad I acted first then figured it out.

Richard Branson was in massive debt for the first fifteen years of Virgin, always getting letters from the bank asking him how he was going to pay for everything. Even in debt, he just kept buying more assets and signing more artists. Somehow he figured it all out, because he had to. To this day, he's creating a space tourism business without knowing how it will all come together. He acts first then he figures it out because he has to.

I wish the universe worked differently. I wish that you could plan to do things and then magically make time and money to do them. It would feel a lot safer. But unfortunately, I don't see that happening for anyone I know. The people I know over-commit themselves then figure it all out as it unfolds.

Earlier, I said:

Resources show up after resourcefulness.

The more resourceful you are, the more resources you will have. That's true, but here's the secret that few people share:

Resourcefulness shows up after you make
a commitment, not before.
#kpibook

Prior to committing to something, half of your resourcefulness is working on overtime on why "this is not a good idea." Without a commitment, humans use up too much brain energy on assessment of the idea, the timing, and trying to predict an unpredictable future. When you finally commit to an outcome, you free up gallons of energy to become more resourceful in following through.

Commit to a big goal, literally sign yourself up to some sort of deadline or external commitment, and then start filling in the blanks as you go.

DON'T WORK FOR THE CLEARING

Becoming a Key Person of Influence doesn't happen for most people because they are waiting for "the clearing." They think that "one day" they will have the time, money, and focus to get something done. So they keep working toward making a clearing rather than going for what they want.

There is no clearing. It never comes. You will be an elderly person in a nursing home and finally you will realize that if you'd just gone for what you wanted, you would have had it. A "clearing" is not a goal. Bite off more than you can chew and then figure it out as you go. If you were any good at creating a clearing in your life, you would have had one by now. When was the last time you actually arrived at "the perfect time and place with all the time and money you needed"? It's a fairy tale.

If you suddenly realize that the most important thing you could be doing for your success is to write a book, then don't put it off. If you know in your heart of hearts that you should be starting a business, then go start it. If it's time to sell your business, then sell it. When something is important you should begin it now rather than waiting for all the circumstances to be perfect. There's never enough time, there's never enough money, there's never a perfect plan—that's life. Move forward anyway.

After you begin a big project you'll find the time and the money. You'll watch less TV, you'll spot a JV opportunity, you'll make more sales, you'll attract a great partner. It all starts after you start.

If you are wrong about your idea, very rarely is the downside catastrophic. In past civilisations, people who had bad ideas died. They were eaten by bears, burned at the stake, tortured to death, or worse. Today, the absolute worst thing that most people fear is the feeling of being labelled a failure. People's worst nightmare is getting embarrassed because their idea didn't work out the way they thought it would. At worst, they may lose some time and some startup capital. Imagine trying to explain that to your ancestors. They faced wars, plagues, and disasters to create a better world and you're not taking full advantage of all it has to offer? You owe it to them to be braver and make some bold moves to achieve your dreams.

You have virtually no downside in perfecting your pitch, writing your book, producing a product, building a profile, and talking to some people about a partnership.

The upside, however, is *awesome.*

WHAT TO LOOK FORWARD TO NEXT

Remember why you are becoming a Key Person of Influence. Keep focused on your big game and why you want to win.

When you are a Key Person of Influence you don't chase;
great opportunities find you.
#kpimethod

Recognition, lucrative deals, recurring income, and other exciting opportunities are commonplace for KPIs. These things are nearly impossible for people who are not yet a Key Person of Influence in their industry.

Here are some tangible things to expect once you are a KPI:

Publicity and media—the media are always looking for expert opinions, feature stories, and case studies. Once you are a KPI, start talking to the media and letting them know what you are up to in the world. Send journalists your book with your bio. When they have a relevant story, they will think of you.

Speaking at events—one speaking opportunity can generate seriously valuable opportunities if done correctly. Remember that speaking opportunities go to KPIs, not great speakers. By the time you have hit the five main outcomes set out in this book, speaking opportunities will have already started to find you.

Directorships—many companies are willing to pay sizable fees, or even equity, to have an established Key Person of Influence as a member of their board.

Your own membership group—as a KPI, you can put together a membership group. Either online or at a live venue these groups can be a great source of income as well as a constant stream of opportunities. Start inviting people to come and join you. You will be amazed at how fast your group can grow.

Subscribers—as a KPI, you can easily have an inner circle of subscribers who pay for premium content or contact with you. I know several KPIs who make over six-figure profits from their subscriber groups and their subscribers love them for it.

Random surprises—KPIs get invited on fun vacations, they get sent free gifts, they get invites to be VIP guests at events and many other fun surprises show up unannounced.

Be sure to keep your eyes on the prize. The reason you are doing this is because all the best opportunities go to KPIs. As a KPI, you will have more fun, make more money, and enjoy more recognition.

If you don't become a KPI, you will get stuck chasing revenue, spend too much time searching for (half-decent) opportunities, and forever feel undervalued.

THE POWER OF MOMENTUM AND THE LAW OF INERTIA

I hated learning physics at school. I remember thinking: what a completely pointless subject. What possible use will I have for this in the future?

Then I saw these two rules of the universe:

Rule 1: The Law of Inertia—An object at rest will stay at rest, until acted upon by an outside force.

And its opposite:

Rule 2: The Law of Momentum—An object in motion will stay in motion, until it meets a resisting force.

These two universal laws have stuck with me since school and reminded me that when I feel the spark to do something, I should act on it straight away. Momentum is too precious to lose. It's a gift that comes far too rarely.

If you feel compelled to act, then go for it. As you get going, you will find that you gather pace and you get enormous amounts accomplished. Often I am happy to sit up until 3am working on something, just so I don't break the momentum.

Of course, if you don't act you become governed by the law of inertia. You become an object at rest, destined to stay at rest until you get a big kick up the butt. Far too often the outside force that gets you to eventually act comes in the form of pain. You realize that you've not achieved any of your goals in two years. You lose a job. You lose a client. You lose a relationship.

Inertia weighs you down and it takes more and more effort to get moving. Momentum is the feeling of being in flow. It's a rush and it's the domain of creativity.

Why am I telling you this?

Because if you have read this far, then deep down inside something is telling you that you are ready to establish yourself as a Key Person of Influence. You have an important pitch to share, you have an amazing book in you, you have a valuable product to produce and you have a worthy message to spread to the world, and others want to partner with you to add more value and reach more people.

You live in a remarkable time in history. It's time to stretch and make the most of it. It's time to invest time, energy, and money into doing the highest-value activities for you. It won't be easy, but it will be worth it.

You've read this book for a reason and that reason is to act. You're here to do it, not to learn about it. Enough with the learning: now is your time to become the Key Person of Influence in your industry.

KPI CLIENT CASE STUDIES

MIKE SYMES

When I first met Mike Symes, he was already successful. He had founded a Marketing Consultancy that specialized in assisting Financial Services companies. He wasn't short of business, but still had to go looking for his new clients.

Mike wanted to take things up a level. He wanted to be priced in the premium end of the market (a well-justified position) and he wanted clients chasing him rather than the traditional method of pitching for new business.

Mike signed up to the KPI Program in April 2010 and immediately had a breakthrough in the way he explained the value he delivers to a client. Rather than saying "I have a financial marketing agency," Mike began telling clients that he "works with Financial Services companies to ignite their brands, illuminate their points of difference, and enable their messages to spread like wildfire, leaving them and their customers feeling inspired" (Pitch).

He then set to work on his book, *Find Your Firebrand*, in which he was able to consolidate his twenty-five years of industry experience into a powerful manuscript (Publish). In doing so, he was able to uncover and explore his unique Intellectual Property. Mike discovered that he had a lot more value to share than he had previously acknowledged.

Next Mike produced a new website and a highly valuable brand assessment tool which could allow people all over the world to access his unique take on Financial Services Branding (Product).

With newfound clarity and scalability, Mike wasted no time in raising his profile online. This resulted in him being appointed as the Chairman of a highly prestigious industry body (Profile). Mike was also able to form joint ventures and partnerships with key industry players (Partnerships).

With all of this in place, Mike noticed a clear shift in the amount of new business that was finding him. In one instance the CEO of one of the UK's largest banks was excited to have the opportunity to sit down over coffee with Mike to discuss the future of their brand.

In a six-month period, Mike Symes went from being a very successful marketing consultant to a Key Person of Influence in his field. He went from being great at pitching for new business to having people pitch to him to become a client. Mike widened his scope to deliver value worldwide and distilled his unique ideas into valuable Intellectual Property. He recognized the mountain of value he was already standing on and is now producing at a whole new level.

Watch the video of Mike Symes sharing his experience of the KPI Accelerator at: www.dent.community

PAUL FOWLER

Paul Fowler has spent a lifetime fascinated by flying. His earliest memories are of building cardboard wings and trying to take flight from the roof of the garden shed. As a teenager he started parachuting, and eventually enrolled into the Army as a paratrooper. Paul's passion then led him to become a pilot, and he spent years flying all over the world.

Even after being forced into an early retirement through illness, Paul still couldn't keep away from planes. He took himself down to the local flying club and started working there to try and rescue the club from going broke.

At the end of twelve months Paul did a deal to buy the Oxfordshire Flying Club and Flight School, and for the first time ever he was a business owner with something he could get passionate about.

His health improved, as did the health of the flight school. Paul had begun to channel his lifetime passion into a business that had wings.

Despite his passion for the business, he did hit a ceiling after the third year in the business. The club grew popular with flying fanatics but something was stopping it from growing to the size it needed to be if this was going to cover the bills and pay Paul a wage.

For the next two years Paul struggled to figure out what would make his beloved flight school really get off the ground. He attended marketing bootcamps, business networking events, and pored over books on marketing and leadership. Nothing seemed to be working, though; the business was flying on one engine.

Then in mid-2010, Paul heard about the Key Person of Influence strategy. He had never even thought about the idea that he could make a name for himself in aviation. "The industry is so big—it employs millions of people—I never dreamed that I could become a Key Person or have any Influence; the idea never crossed my mind until I heard Daniel Priestley talking about it," says Paul.

After joining the program, his first step was to identify a micro-niche and learn how to do a perfect pitch. "I've always dreamed of owning a Spitfire aircraft and I guessed other people would want to fly one as well, so I decided to go for my lifetime dream and create the Spitfire Project," Paul says.

At the Perfect Pitch workshop, Paul developed his idea and arrived at a clear way to explain it to others. "Mike Harris told me to get out and start pitching it to see how people respond," says Paul. "He also said I should go looking for people who say that it will never work because they will help to identify where the pitch needs to be stronger."

Three months later, as a result of pitching the idea to anyone who would listen, Paul was crystal clear on his pitch. He then set about writing an article for the number-one industry magazine, *Pilot*. He phoned the editor and pitched his article and the editor gave Paul a double-page spread dedicated to the Spitfire Project on the spot, even before he had finished his pitch.

Within months Paul was being invited to speak around the country about his project and was gathering interested parties who wanted to invest in the iconic plane and take lessons to learn to fly it.

Off the back of the article, Paul was approached by the BBC and Channel 4 to discuss making a documentary on the project.

With so much buzz being created, Paul knew he needed to start focusing on productizing the business. He set about creating a "Zero to Hero" program that would fast-track a private pilot from beginner level through to flying their own Spitfire. It was a bold move, but it received a lot of immediate interest.

He also began putting his Flight Briefings onto audio and video so that people could learn from home and share their excitement with friends.

> *"It's funny, we do dozens of Flight Briefings each week, but until KPI I'd never even thought of them as potential products. I'm guessing most businesses are the same; they probably have more opportunities under their noses than they think."*

Next, Paul worked to build an online social media profile for his flight school and his Spitfire Project. "I'm blown away at how many people are now reading our blogs and watching our videos on the web."

Finally, with all this in place, Paul was able to begin doing JVs and partnerships with other businesses in the industry. Some of his first deals involved having the flight school promoted to lists of over 10,000 people as well as a win/win partnership with a local hotel.

"I now feel like I am on track to be a Key Person of Influence in my Industry. KPI gave me a map to follow and helped me to see where I was on the map. Then it gave me the strategy to move forward to where I wanted to be. My flight school is finally taking off and I'm feeling good about being in the captain's seat," says Paul.

Watch the video of Paul Fowler sharing his experience of the KPI Accelerator at: www.dent.community

JANE MALYON

Jane Malyon is lovely and nice! Everyone says so because she has such a wonderful manner and warm disposition.

When we met Jane she had come from a thirty-year background in hospitality and catering and had also been in business as a coach and trainer. Her niche was centred on resolving conflict, using your best etiquette under pressure and having better manners.

As Jane crafted her pitch, she began to realize she had a deep burning desire to bring the best out in people. Not just some people but thousands of them. She wasn't sure how this would happen but she knew something big was starting to stir.

Jane wrote the book *Play Nicely* and was forced to dive deep into her core ideas and philosophies on what makes people behave at their best and win people over with rapport and kindness rather than by authority.

During the KPI process, when Jane worked on her products she hit a roadblock. She explored voicing a CD, creating a training program, and even developing software. Nothing seemed to deliver the special experience she knew she wanted to create. Then, after randomly meeting an elderly lady who had become too frail to travel to the Savoy for her favourite annual treat of elegant afternoon tea, Jane had a flash of inspiration and imagined chilled delivery of a high-quality gift box containing ready-to-enjoy high tea and scones.

It was perfect. For years Jane had entertained family and friends at the Savoy or Ritz Carlton for afternoon tea and she was always delighted at the way her guests would naturally be at their best. The experience was natural, fun, and filled with rapport—and the conversations encouraged collaboration and togetherness. It was everything she wanted to deliver to the world, and it worked by magic.

To build her Profile, Jane set an audacious goal to win a Guinness World Record. She called in all sorts of favours and remarkably set the world record for the largest gathering in one place, all enjoying English cream tea.

She was featured on the BBC, in newspapers, magazines, and blogs, and as a speaker at large conferences.

With the added profile, Jane noted that orders started to fly in and so did offers for partnership. People didn't just want to buy her product, they also wanted to license her brand.

Within two years of launch, The English Cream Tea Company has shipped thousands of products all over the UK and built a brand that is set to expand globally.

Jane's products are being used as gifts to say "Thank you," "I'm sorry," and even "A substitute for a hug," as one loyal customer said.

This new business combines the best parts of Jane's story: catering, hospitality, coaching, and a desire to bring out the best in people. Jane's vision of inspiring people to play nicely is fast becoming a reality.

Watch the video of Jane Malyon sharing her experience of the KPI Accelerator at: www.dent.community

DARREN FINKELSTEIN

Darren and I stood eye to eye staring each other down. He was arguing with me that the KPI Method wouldn't work for him.

Darren sells boats, or at least that's what he was telling me at the time. He didn't believe that writing a book would make any difference and he didn't think it was possible to create any products.

After a short, sharp exchange I said to him, "You're not in the boat sales business you're in the boat *ownership* business." He instantly got it: his business shouldn't be built around a single transaction; his business should be built around the entire experience of owning a boat.

Darren co-founded his Melbourne-based business because of his belief that "life's better with a boat," but after ten years in business he had lost touch with the original intention of his business.

After reconnecting with the "joy of boat ownership" Darren suddenly got a flood of new energy and inspiration.

When people spoke to him, he started talking about all the fun his clients have on boats. He talked about how the kids put down the PlayStations and really connected with their parents on the boat. He talked about special boating adventures that people had and how many owners feel completely free when they're out at sea. He no longer pitches the sale; instead he talks from the heart about the experiences an owner gets.

His book was written and published in just 200 days—*Honey, Let's Buy a Boat!* is now selling copies all over the world and it tells the full story of what owning a boat is all about. His book covers the purchase, the upkeep, the enjoyment, and the sale or upgrade.

Darren has added almost a dozen new products and services to his business. Under the new umbrella of boat ownership his company now services, refuels, restocks, washes, and valet parks their clients' boats. They also teach people how to become better boat owners and have more enjoyment on the water. This has added an uplift to Darren's business that is unheard of in his industry.

After the release of his book, building a profile came easy. Darren was featured in the media and prominent magazines read by his market. He has spoken all over Australia to crowds of boat owners and he's become a trusted commentator in his industry. Most of this activity has ended up online and he's all over the front page of Google when you start searching for him or his business.

Darren loves growing his business through partnerships. He focuses on creating win/win alliances with others in the industry who are making life better with boats. Darren even turned down a major opportunity because it didn't feel like a true partnership that was beyond a fast transaction. As Darren says, "If it's not good long term, it's not good short term."

Darren is in his zone now and looking at ways to grow his business. Rather than chasing the next sale, he's advancing the cause of enjoyable boat ownership. Darren and I catch up at least a few times a year and I always remind him of that conversation where he rediscovered his passion for boat ownership. After all, if you don't own a boat it's wise to be friends with a guy who has a busy marina.

Watch the video of Darren Finkelstein sharing his experience of the KPI Accelerator at: www.dent.community

JACQUIE SHARPLES

Some people are pretty fit, but Jacquie Sharples is an athlete. She's a pole vaulter, an athletics master, and a damn good runner. A few times I've braved the chance to run with Jacquie and I've always marvelled at how she can be chatting away to me while I'm barely able to breathe.

Her fitness comes from a deep love of the human body. She understands fitness and the relationship between food, movement, mindset, and maintenance. Very few people are tuned into the body the way she is. With such a deep love of health and fitness, Jacquie had always flirted with the idea of running a business that matched her passion.

She'd always enjoyed teaching friends and colleagues about fitness, and debunking the fad diets and workouts that come flooding through the media. As an engineer, however, she wasn't sure she could jump the hurdles required to make a business successful.

Jacquie began with her pitch and discovered that people responded well to her once she had crafted her message. She communicated with clarity, credibility, and real passion every time she got asked the question "What do you do?" Pretty soon she started feeling more comfortable talking about her fitness business instead of her job.

Next she set about writing her book. Rather than a conventional book in the non-fiction genre, Jacquie wrote *If Your Body Could Talk*, a series of letters written to you from your body. Each letter explains how the body is dealing with your daily decisions. Many of the letters are written as a plea from the body to have a better relationship with its owner. It's fun, engaging, inspiring, and informative.

The products started to take shape when we set Jacquie the challenge of creating a perfect brochure for a product she'd love her friends to buy. She created the "Love your body, love your life" program as a twelve-week challenge for corporate women to break their sedentary lifestyle. Within a few months, she'd made enough sales to earn more each month than she was making in her corporate job.

As predictable as clockwork, a great book and a hot product generated attention, and soon she was getting press and other PR.

She built her profile online and started to see new enquiries hitting her Facebook page every week.

Finally, Jacquie started looking for partnerships. She wanted people to promote her and her book to their contacts. She discovered that many companies had databases full of corporate women and were happy to set up strategic alliances to help more people to love their bodies and love their lives.

Today Jacquie is looking pretty fit for business as well as for the running track. She's gained strength and power behind her brand and she can leap confidently into her new career as a fitness entrepreneur. Jacquie is a Key Person of Influence and is having a greater impact on people than she'll ever know.

Watch the video of Jacquie Sharples sharing her experience of the KPI Accelerator at: www.dent.community

JUSTINE PRIESTLEY

It seems strange to write about my sister as a success story. To a skeptic, it would seem a little biased, but in reality I'm not only a proud big brother but also an admirer of the way she does business.

I'm eight years older than Justine and I've always tried to set a good example of how to make the most of any situation life presents. I've always tried to encourage her to believe that anything is possible.

When my sister told me she wanted to be an actress, however, my heart sank. I imagined her lining up with thousands of young, talented aspirants at casting call after casting call. My understanding of the industry was that a lot had to happen in order to break into the industry and most actors were struggling with finances and confidence as they tried to enter into a very closed industry.

I had many conversations with my sister and we eventually planned out a path for her to follow. Rather than going down the usual route of acting schools and casting calls, we explored the idea of her setting up her own media and production company.

At the age of twenty-two, Justine founded her own company, Really Bright Media, and started following the KPI Method. She developed a pitch where she was able to win business every month producing videos for businesses that they could use online. Her pitch was strong and she soon became so busy that she had to start hiring others to keep up with demand.

Together with her partner Andy, she wrote the book *Brighter*, which described how businesses could use social media video to raise their profile. The book was a perfect tool for demonstrating credibility and helping win more clients.

Next they worked on creating products and service offerings that were unique in London. They created a Social Media Action Group for their clients who wanted to produce something every month. They created different filming packages for different purposes, and each package had its own brochures, benefits, and pricing.

Justine is a natural speaking on stage, and she used her skills to build her profile. She started speaking at events and conferences. She was even flown internationally to take part in several conferences around Europe.

The final piece was partnerships. Justine and Andy embraced the idea by doing joint ventures with my company and several others who could recommend their services. There are also several promising partnerships in place that will take the business far and wide in the years to come.

So what happened to the acting career—did she give it up? Certainly not! Fortunately, her film production company means that she's on camera almost every week as a presenter, and her company regularly enters film competitions and has won international awards. Justine is becoming very well-known in her industry as an actor and a film maker.

Along this path, Justine has discovered that many famous actors started out by producing their own films and that others who started out the traditional way have also crossed over to start a media company later in their career. This is an entirely valid way to break into a tough industry and to always ensure she's backed up with ample opportunities that don't rely upon the fickle finger of fate.

As it turns out, there are many paths up a mountain and sometimes it's worth approaching things side on. Despite being in her mid-twenties, Justine is already a Key Person of Influence in the London media and film scene and showing all the signs of having a really bright future ahead.

But of course I would say that.

MORE SUCCESS STORIES

We've compiled over one hundred video case studies of people who have used the Key Person of Influence method to become more highly valued and highly paid. To see people sharing their own stories, visit: www.dent.community

AFTERWORD

Congratulations on reading this book and taking steps toward being a truly connected, highly regarded Key Person of Influence in the industry you love.

This book had clear themes in it. You read about developing your pitch and a micro-niche, writing and publishing content, making products, building your profile, and doing joint ventures and partnerships.

All of these ideas are important—was there something else you noticed?

Did you notice a recurring theme that kept coming up for you? Did you connect the dots and see something you weren't expecting?

The book was only a tool to spot this deeper theme; something that's personal to you and something only you could see.

When you do spot your theme, you will discover that your future is clear, your past was perfect, and you are present to the opportunities that are all around you.

After you spot your hidden theme:

*You will get a burst of energy; you may sit up all night
writing, recording, producing, and playing… and when
morning comes, you're still not tired. You'll feel good
because everything clicked into place.*

That's because everything was for a reason. Nothing was out of order, nothing was superfluous, and nothing came along to hold you back. It was all there for the purpose of letting you discover what that theme is.

You may need to read this book again, though. It's not the content that really matters, it's the story behind the pages. More than that, it's the chapters that are coming next that matter most.

Of course, the chapter that comes next may be at the beginning of this book as you keep looking, or it may be the chapter that you write for yourself. The important thing is that you find it, and it's yours to share.

THE KEY PERSON OF INFLUENCE ACCELERATOR

The Key Person of Influence Accelerator is designed for established entrepreneurs, leaders, and service-based business owners. It helps them to implement the principles and best practices outlined in this book to establish themselves as the obvious "go-to" choice in their market or niche.

It is designed to help you project-manage the implementation of the "five Ps," tap into a peer group, and learn from world-class mentors.

Thousands of people around the world have used the accelerator to dramatically shift the performance of their businesses and their lives.

This book stresses the importance of high-quality implementation and the accelerator is designed as a predictable journey for reinventing yourself or your team to become more highly valued in your industry.

The program runs in cities all over the world. In each city, groups of up to seventy-five entrepreneurs are selected to participate in the twelve-month accelerator program. The process is fast-paced and results-orientated. It's about implementation, not just ideas.

The Key Person of Influence Accelerator provides resources to speed up your progress. After working with thousands of people, we've discovered the strategies that create results much faster than trying to do this all on your own. Our method is independently recognized by the Institute of Leadership and Management, Europe's largest management training certification body.

The mentors on the program are celebrated local heroes of business and entrepreneurship. They are typically people who have built multi-million (and in some cases even multi-billion) -dollar companies), CEOs of big businesses and charities, best-selling authors, and thought leaders.

The mentors share their real-world experiences and give feedback to the participants in small group environments.

Participants consistently tell us that the program was a catalyst for dramatic improvements far exceeding what they could have accomplished on their own.

You can learn more about the Accelerator here: www.dent.community

NEXT STEPS

You're a lot closer than you may think to breaking through to the inner circle of your industry. To learn how you can apply this methodology to your own business, here are some next steps.

1. A GLOBAL ONLINE COMMUNITY

Join the Oversubscribed Facebook community to stay connected to best practices, resources, and a community of entrepreneurs who are choosing to stand out and scale up their businesses.

Both the authors regularly post inside the group and fuel the global conversation among established founders who are building their brands and scaling their businesses.

www.oversubscribed.group

2. ONLINE TRAINING

Dive deeper into the principles outlined in this book by joining our free online training masterclass in becoming a Key Person of Influence in your industry. If you feel like you're constantly having to chase new business, are handcuffed to service delivery, and have no predictable way to generate leads and sales, then this training provides a roadmap to break through those challenges.

www.kpiwebclass.com

3. BENCHMARK YOUR CURRENT INDUSTRY INFLUENCE

We created the Key Person of Influence Scorecard to allow you to benchmark your current strengths and weaknesses in each step of the KPI Method and know what to improve. This test has been taken by more than 50,000 entrepreneurs around the world, and what we've discovered is that success in business is highly correlated to your level of influence. When you've completed the scorecard, it gives you a personalized report with recommendations on what to focus on. It's free to use and takes less than ten minutes to complete.

www.scalemyinfluence.com

4. APPLY FOR THE KEY PERSON OF INFLUENCE ACCELERATOR

Every year Dent selects a group of up to seventy-five entrepreneurs through its intensive twelve-month accelerator in each of its locations.

Before Dent accepts an entrepreneur into its accelerator programs, there is an evaluation done through a Dent Strategy Session. Dent has run these sessions with more than 5000 entrepreneurs globally and they typically take place in small groups in each city Dent where operates.

These sessions are designed to uncover the opportunities for you to apply the KPI Method into your business and assess your suitability for selection into one of Dent's accelerator programs.

To learn more and attend one of these sessions, go to:
www.kpidiagnostic.com

THE AUTHORS

DANIEL PRIESTLEY

Daniel founded his first company in 2002 in Australia at the age of twenty-one. Before he was twenty-five, he and his business partners had grown a national business turning over several million dollars.

In 2006, Daniel moved from Australia to launch a new venture in London. Arriving with only a suitcase and a credit card, Daniel set up a new venture and grew it to seven-figure revenues in under two years. In the process, he became a leading figure in his industry and had the opportunity to be mentored personally by some of the world's top entrepreneurs and leaders.

Daniel's entrepreneurial career has included starting, building, buying, financing, and selling businesses. He is now regarded as one of the world's top professional speakers on business and entrepreneurship.

Today Daniel works with his lifelong friends and business partners to build global entrepreneurship and leadership programs through the Dent Accelerators. Dent reinvents traditional businesses using a unique approach to personal branding and leveraging technology. He is also active in fund-raising for charity and working with the leadership teams.

Daniel is the author of three other best-selling books: *Entrepreneur Revolution*, *Oversubscribed*, and *24 Assets*.

MIKE REID

Mike co-founded Dent Global, a business accelerator that provides training and implementation for entrepreneurial businesses. To date, Dent has worked with over 3000 ambitious entrepreneurs with six to seven-figure revenue businesses globally.

Since his early 20s, Mike has run over twenty large-scale promotional campaigns—including business conferences of 300–600 people filled by over 150 channel partners. These campaigns have contributed to Dent and the Key Person of Influence Accelerator being recognized as one of the fastest-growing companies in Australia (BRW & Smart Company 2014.)

After leaving Dent's Australian operations and taking six months' sabbatical to travel the world in 2018, Mike is expanding Dent's business into Canada, helping Canadian entrepreneurs to stand out, scale up, and make an even bigger impact with what they do.

Mike is also the host of the *Dichotomy Podcast*—a show dedicated to helping entrepreneurs navigate the dichotomies they face in their lives, so they can build a business and a life that gives them more of what they truly want.